D1210180

THE TEACHER PORTFOLIO

HOW TO ORDER THIS BOOK

BY PHONE: 800-233-9936 or 717-291-5609, 8AM–5PM Eastern Time

BY FAX: 717-295-4538

BY MAIL: Order Department
Technomic Publishing Company, Inc.
851 New Holland Avenue, Box 3535
Lancaster, PA 17604, U.S.A.

BY CREDIT CARD: American Express, VISA, MasterCard

PERMISSION TO PHOTOCOPY–POLICY STATEMENT

THE
TEACHER
PORTFOLIO

A STRATEGY FOR PROFESSIONAL DEVELOPMENT AND EVALUATION

James E. Green, Ph.D.
The University of Tulsa

Sheryl O'Sullivan Smyser, Ed.D.
University of Redlands

TECHNOMIC
PUBLISHING CO., INC.
LANCASTER · BASEL

The Teacher Portfolio
a TECHNOMIC® publication

Published in the Western Hemisphere by
Technomic Publishing Company, Inc.
851 New Holland Avenue, Box 3535
Lancaster, Pennsylvania 17604 U.S.A.

Distributed in the Rest of the World by
Technomic Publishing AG
Missionsstrasse 44
CH-4055 Basel, Switzerland

Printed in the United States of America
10 9 8 7 6 5 4 3

Main entry under title:
    The Teacher Portfolio: A Strategy for Professional Development and Evaluation

A Technomic Publishing Company book
Bibliography: p.

Library of Congress Catalog Card No. 95-61713
ISBN No. 1-56676-371-1

CONTENTS

NEARLY everyone today advocates education reform. Rarely is there a political campaign where the contestants do not soundly flog the system and propose that "something be done." Teachers often know from experience that "something" usually appears in the form of additional universal mandates or top-down, one-size-fits-all solutions. Consequently, the professional development that is often part of legislated reform typically is geared to uniform expectations and mass audiences, and often has resulted in teacher cynicism rather than improvement.

Many education reform programs do not result in the startling progress they promise because they fail to recognize that fundamental change in education does not occur without the renewal and professional development of teachers. More importantly, renewal and professional development will not occur without fundamental change in how we assess teaching and guide the process of growth.

Neither teacher renewal nor teacher assessment will fit into a bureaucratic model. As teachers we differ from one another. Our schools and classrooms differ. Our grade levels, subjects, and pupils differ. The way one teacher works with pupils will differ from the way another might, yet both may be highly effective. Moreover, we continue to grow professionally only if we make a personal commitment to grow.

Just as *reform* is not something that can be done to a school, *renewal* or *assessment* is not something that can be done to a teacher. Renewal and assessment always have been and always will be deeply personal processes. Renewal, which means the process of making new again, is a matter of individual motivation on the part of the teacher. Only the individual can decide what it will take to invigorate his or her teaching. Reflection and introspection will be necessary to discern the teaching aspects that have gone stale and need to be freshened, and only changes motivated from within can have any hope of producing a "new" teacher.

While renewal must come from within the teacher, this does not mean it needs to be an isolated or lonely journey. Guides and helpers along the way can make the whole process more fruitful. This is where assessment becomes important. "Assess" originally came from Latin meaning "to sit beside" or "assist in the office of judge." Today we have lost much of this original meaning when we think of the term "assessment," but if we recapture this early intent we can understand assessment in a totally new way. Assessment would no longer be something an outsider, usually the principal, does *to* a teacher. Instead, it would become a cooperative activity between professionals. The teacher would begin and direct the journey through personal reflection, and the mentor would "sit beside" the teacher offering a fresh perspective and new ideas.

If we are to have genuine reform in our schools we must first have fundamental change in ourselves as teachers. Individually. One at a time. We must change at the personal level our habits of mind and spirit of heart. We must begin looking at ourselves and how we teach in different ways, and we must begin acting on what we learn. In short, we teachers need to renew ourselves if we are going to have any kind of meaningful reform in our schools.

Now, think for a moment how we come by our feedback as teachers. It comes from parents, and it is often nonsupportive. It comes from our pupils — sometimes it is supportive, and sometimes it is not. It comes from our supervisors, principals usually, and then it is all too often either infrequent or superficial. Rarely does it come from our peers — other teachers. And, here is the irony. We find ourselves insulated from the very persons who are best equipped to help us and support us.

An additional irony is that we rarely ask ourselves for feedback on our own teaching. The *teaching portfolio* as a strategy for professional development is based on the premise that the best assessment is self-assessment. Teachers are more likely to act on what they find out about themselves. The principal's check marks and several paragraphs of summary generated from a one-hour observation (out of the thousand or so a teacher spends teaching in a school year) will not produce the kind of personal reflection that precedes the interior change necessary for renewal.

As a strategy for professional development, the teaching portfolio is based on other premises as well. The process of planning and creating a teaching portfolio as we have described presupposes that interior change occurs only as a consequence of self-reflection. And, professional dialogue in a climate of candor and trust is crucial to supporting that process of self-reflection. With these elements as a foundation — self-assessment, self-reflection, and professional dialogue — the teaching portfolio becomes a radically new concept in teacher evaluation and professional development.

We have set out to give teachers and administrators a practical guide to using the teaching portfolio as a strategy for professional development and evaluation. Accordingly, we have tried to stick to real situations and real examples rather than elucidate theory as we explain how to plan and create a portfolio. Also, we hoped to avoid a cookbook approach to developing a teaching portfolio or implementing teaching portfolios in a school. Ultimately teachers and administrators have to find their individual ways in their own classrooms and schools. Instead, we attempted to show some concrete applications of guidelines and offer suggestions teachers and administrators may follow. Our hope is that teacher evaluation will become a process of self-assessment, which we hope will invite the professional dialogue and self-reflection necessary for renewal and continuing professional development.

JIM GREEN AND SHERI SMYSER
August 1995

CHAPTER 1

Teacher Evaluation Today: What It's Like and What It Could Be

OVERVIEW

IN most schools today teacher evaluation is conducted much in the same way it was a half century ago. The principal makes a couple of observations; collects some second-hand information from students, parents, or other teachers; and then reports the evaluation on an official form. The principal and teacher may hold a conference or two, and that is it. Once it's over, it's over—at least until the next year.

Teaching portfolios promise to transform teacher evaluation into a reflective process for the teacher—one that uses peer mentoring and self-evaluation—so that professional development becomes the main purpose.

ORGANIZING PRINCIPLES

- Teaching occurs in diverse settings.
- Effective teachers may have different styles of teaching.
- Collegiality enhances professional growth in teachers.
- Self-reflection is necessary to improve teaching.
- Evaluation of teachers should lead to professional growth.

WHAT IS WRONG WITH EVALUATION TODAY?

Think of the best teacher you ever had. Now, try to describe what that teacher was like. More than likely each of you described very different kinds of teachers.

When we try to identify the characteristics of good teachers – the ones who had the most influence on our lives – we amaze one another with the variety we find. We use words like *caring, tough, inspiring, demanding, creative,* and *well-organized,* often in the same sentences, but we are struck by the dissimilar ways we describe our best teachers. We are also a little perplexed by the ambiguous and even contradictory nature of our descriptions. How is it that we include one teacher whom we remember as tough and demanding in the same list as one whom we thought of as nurturing and caring? How can a teacher who is spontaneous and creative be as successful as one who is exceedingly well-organized and detail oriented? Typically, we shrug our shoulders and agree that good teaching is, indeed, a paradox.

The paradoxical nature of successful teaching continues to frustrate both teachers and administrators. However, the problem is not so much one of recognizing good teaching, for we all know when we are in the same classroom as a master. The problem comes when we try to evaluate teaching. In addition, we are confounded when we try to use evaluation as a way to encourage the professional growth of teachers.

Why is evaluation so difficult? Why do so many teachers today roll their eyes when you mention that their annual evaluation has been scheduled? Probably for several reasons.

Current Practices Utilize a Single Paradigm

First, evaluation in most schools is a one-size-fits-all process. Even if separate forms are used for elementary and secondary schools and the forms are the product of extensive teacher input, the process homogenizes the professional skills, individual traits, and personal values that will vary among really effective teachers. Teachers will be the first to tell you that teaching is too sublime to be reduced to a few descriptors that fit on one page. Yet we still evaluate teachers with checklists that attempt to do just this! A typical evaluation form does not acknowledge that teaching can be informed by various theories or that students will respond to teachers who employ various styles of teaching. Figure 1.1 lists examples of typical items from teacher evaluation forms.

Moreover, learning happens in very different kinds of classrooms, with very different kinds of pupils. "Teaches the objectives through a variety of methods" does not begin to describe how a high school

> **TYPICAL EVALUATION ITEMS**
>
> Teaches objectives through a variety of methods
>
> Follows the adopted curriculum
>
> Maintains effective classroom discipline
>
> Classroom is neat in appearance

Figure 1.1 Typical evaluation items.

mathematics teacher approaches a ninth-grade applied math class for a dozen children with learning disabilities versus a class that prepares college-bound seniors for an Advanced Placement examination in calculus. Teaching is too diverse and the places where teaching occurs are too varied for traditional methods of evaluation to be useful for teachers.

Current Practices Lack Collegiality

Next, teaching is often a lonely profession. Although opportunities for team teaching have existed for more than two decades, most teachers practice their profession in relative isolation. Curriculum-planning and textbook-adoption meetings provide some chance for teachers to discuss students and learning in a professional context, but these discussions are intended to address issues or solve problems that are general to the school or the district. Rare is the chance that teachers meet as peers — one on one — to talk about the meaning of good teaching and to discuss in a supportive climate their individual strengths and weaknesses. The dynamics of schools do not encourage teachers to discuss teaching with one another. When they are with other teachers, they are in groups with whom they may not want to bare their professional souls. When they are with a principal in an evaluation conference, the tendency is to hope for a glowing evaluation and not reveal uncertainties. As a result, teachers are left to go it alone, often when they most need to reflect on their own teaching and what they could be doing to improve it.

Current Practices Lack Self-Reflection

The rarity of personal reflection is another reason why teachers frequently are cynical about current approaches to evaluation. A supervisor's check mark to indicate that a teacher "teaches the objectives through a variety of methods" some of the time or most of the time does not cause that teacher to reflect. Rather, it only causes a teacher to agree or disagree. Or worse, it causes the teacher to resent the supervisor who attempts to make such a judgment from insufficient evidence.

Self-reflection is the point of departure for professional growth. A teacher must make an honest inventory of personal strengths and weaknesses before professional growth can occur. It is not something that someone can do to the teacher or for the teacher. Current practices in teacher evaluation start with someone, usually the principal, telling the teacher what needs to happen. It doesn't work!

Current Practices Do Not Direct Professional Growth

Finally, the main purpose of evaluation is to direct further growth. If the evaluation process does not cause someone to learn a new personal insight and use that insight for improvement, then evaluation has failed. However, as teacher evaluation is currently practiced, it seldom directs growth. For the principal, evaluation is often tedious, amounting to completing a form based upon very little actual evidence. For the teacher, the process appears either threatening or superficial, depending on whether the teacher is struggling or thriving. In neither case is the end result of the evaluation a coherent, teacher-directed plan for professional growth.

WHAT MAKES A TEACHING PORTFOLIO A DIFFERENT KIND OF EVALUATION?

Teaching portfolios represent a new approach to evaluating teachers and encouraging their professional growth. Teachers are the first to recognize that teaching and learning go on in very diverse settings with very diverse pupils. In addition, teachers realize that they all have different strengths and weaknesses—that what works for one may not work for another. Reflecting on the different contexts and different personal attributes that make up the real background for teaching and learning—and discussing these differences with other teachers—is the distinguishing feature of a teaching portfolio. When teachers prepare a teaching portfolio, they integrate all aspects of teaching.

Portfolios Give Teaching a Context

If we look at the origin of the word *context*, we find that it means "to weave together." When we use the term in reading and writing, context is how we find the meaning of words or how we hold the meaning of our words together. Well, teaching also has context, and it is the context of teaching that gives it meaning.

Think of all the ways that situations for teaching differ. It's a long list. The type of school community, the age level of pupils, the subject, and the curriculum all shape the context of teaching. In addition, the roles and expectations of teachers change from situation to situation and from teacher to teacher.

For the evaluation of teaching to be meaningful, it must take into account the individual contexts of teachers. Demonstration of content knowledge or general pedagogical knowledge on a test is an incomplete picture of a teacher (Shulman, 1987). A teaching portfolio lets a teacher define good teaching in a specific context.

Portfolios Accommodate Diversity

Teachers and pupils come in all types. Just as we can describe teachers in many different ways, we can describe pupils in many different ways. Cultures, aptitudes, special needs, and individual interests are only a few of the differences that teachers notice in a typical classroom, and they have to teach in ways that reach all the pupils. When teachers prepare teaching portfolios, they can explain how they tailor their teaching to the unique qualities of a particular school or class.

Portfolios Encourage Teachers to Capitalize on Strengths

Good teachers know how to capitalize on their strengths. That is one of the reasons that they are good. However, not every teacher has the same strengths. Indeed, when we remember our very best teachers, we are surprised at how different from one another they really were.

When teachers are evaluated or when they evaluate themselves, the question ought not to be whether they fit the norm for good teachers, but whether they enable pupils to learn. The central question a teacher asks when preparing a teaching portfolio is, "What are the qualities I have as a teacher that enable my pupils to learn?" This question allows for diversity in the way teachers teach and in the way pupils learn.

Portfolios Allow Teachers to Self-Identify Areas for Improvement

Professional development should be something that teachers do for themselves, not something that is done to them. Consequently, the first step in an effective professional development program is for teachers to identify for themselves what they need to change or how they need to grow.

When teachers are told their deficiencies, they are likely to become defensive. Therefore, they are likely to resist attempts to help them improve. However, when they recognize for themselves what they need to do to become better teachers, they are more likely to develop an action plan for change. The teaching portfolio as a tool for staff development is based on the premise that the best knowledge is self-knowledge.

Portfolios Empower Teachers by Making Them Reflective

Self-knowledge requires introspection. The only way teachers can learn about their own strengths and weaknesses as teachers is to reflect, first of all, on the meaning of good teaching and on finding evidence of good teaching. Once a teacher knows what to look for, then the process of self-examination becomes a matter of collecting the evidence. The match, or mismatch, between what a teacher thinks good teaching should be and the evidence of good teaching is the basis for recognizing both teaching strengths and particular areas that need improvement.

A teaching portfolio encourages a teacher to think reflectively about teaching by asking several questions.

- What do I value in teaching?
- What are my goals as a teacher?

- What is the evidence in the way I teach or in the results of my teaching that my teaching reflects my values and that I am accomplishing my goals?
- What are my strengths and weaknesses?
- How do my strengths and weaknesses match up with the kind of teacher I want to be?
- What are my goals for professional growth?

These questions form a paradigm for self-evaluation (see Figure 1.2). A teacher's own values and goals become the basis of the evaluation. The teacher then finds evidence to determine whether his or her teaching reflects these values and meets the desired professional goals. Individual strengths and weaknesses become the focus for that teacher's professional development program.

Self-reflection that is prompted by the preparation of the portfolio is the beginning point for enabling a teacher to be responsible for individual professional development.

Portfolios Empower Teachers by Encouraging Professional Dialogue

Ironically, teachers practice their profession in isolation from one another. True, team teaching can be found in some schools, and committees are common. But, the actual planning, instructing, and evaluating are done as a lone ranger. And, regrettably, most of the teacher-lounge talk is far removed from issues that define good teaching or the evidence of good teaching. Teachers need to talk to teachers if they are to grow professionally.

Many states now have mentoring programs for first-year teachers, and the programs nearly always utilize a mentor teacher—someone with whom a beginning teacher can frankly discuss what is working and what is not working. Effective teachers know that learning to teach is a career-long process, not one that is accomplished in one year, and that all teachers need mentors. Mentoring fosters dialogue between professionals.

When a teacher begins a teaching portfolio, dialogue begins. A teaching portfolio should stimulate and facilitate professional interaction among teachers (Shulman, 1988). When working with a portfolio mentor, a teacher has to discuss what is important in teaching and how good teaching is revealed in the classroom.

Figure 1.2 Paradigm for reflective teaching.

Portfolios Integrate All Aspects of Teaching

How do you break a teacher into separate parts? Teaching is too sublime to be reduced to a list of discrete skills. No one ever heard of a really great teacher who was excellent at planning but weak in other areas. Nor has anyone known a truly outstanding teacher who had mastered classroom management but could not plan or evaluate instruction. A great teacher integrates many skills.

Only when we look at the whole package—everything from a teacher's personal philosophy on teaching and learning to the actual results obtained—do we really begin to understand what makes up an individual teacher. The process of preparing a teaching portfolio demands that a teacher integrate all aspects of teaching. A teaching portfolio ties together the personal history and the personal values of the teacher, the teaching environment, planning skills, classroom management techniques, evaluation skills, creativity, and organizational talents.

RESEARCH ON THE BENEFITS OF TEACHING PORTFOLIOS

The teaching portfolio is proving to be a valuable tool for professional development for solid reasons. Recent research on multiple intelligences, learning styles, and cultural diversity provides ample evidence that teachers must approach instruction from many different angles. Also, research continues to reveal that individual differences occur among highly effective teachers. These changes in the way we think about teaching and learning argue strongly in favor of using teaching portfolios.

Reflective Teaching

Several studies cite the increase of reflective thinking on teaching as a primary benefit of teaching portfolios (Berry, Kisch, Ryan, and Uphoff, 1991; Biddle and Lasley, 1991; Richert, 1990). Richert reported that the use of teaching portfolios with novice teachers resulted in greater specificity of focus on content and pedagogy. The very act of constructing a portfolio was believed to encourage reflection as the student teacher made critical decisions about what items to include.

Integration

Integration of the many content areas and basic pedagogy that teachers must master was reported by Berry et al. (1991); Biddle and Lasley (1991); and Cole et al. (1991). Reporting on the activity of the Ohio Consortium for Portfolio Development, which studied the use of portfolios among students preparing to be teachers, Biddle and Lasley stated that the use of portfolios can integrate the areas of the curriculum by allowing the student to see how ideas are connected. This insight is especially important in connecting content areas to pedagogy.

Collegiality

Another apparent benefit of using teaching portfolios is the encouragement of professional dialogue that is such a vital part of the portfolio development process. Richert (1990) reported that novice teachers often cite the opportunity to engage in conversations about teaching with colleagues as a particularly helpful means of encouraging growth during the first year of teaching. A structured approach for two colleagues to reflect upon their own teaching was also cited as valuable by beginning teachers.

Assessment

A further benefit of using teaching portfolios is their value during assessment procedures. They can be used for a variety of evaluation purposes, including employment interviews (Biddle and Lasley, 1991; Weinberger and Didham, 1987). Weinberger and Didham reported that employers responded favorably to teaching portfolios as part of the interview process.

While teaching portfolios are valuable as an evaluation tool used by others, their use as a self-assessment technique should not be overlooked. Indeed, the value of portfolios as a tool for professional development depends upon their effectiveness for self-assessment. Berry et al. (1991) stressed the usefulness of teaching portfolios for self-assessment and provided strong support for portfolios as a means of involving teachers in their own evaluations.

Changing Concepts of Teaching

The key to professional development is personal change. Teachers grow professionally only when they embrace new ideas and commit to changing the way they look at themselves and teaching. In a study of students preparing to be teachers, Green and Smyser (1995) examined the effects of using teaching portfolios on the meaning that students give basic concepts of teaching. They found that students gave more positive value to the concepts of professional development, reflective thinking, and evaluation of teaching after they were assisted in the development of their teaching portfolios.

National Trends

Some states are beginning to mandate teaching portfolios as part of their teacher induction programs, and many colleges and universities have systematically introduced portfolios as a central element in their teacher education programs. The most notable development in wide-spread use, however, is the assessment process used by the National Board for Professional Teaching Standards (Bradley, 1994). The development of a portfolio is a central feature of the assessment.

SUMMARY

When a group of teachers gathers and the topic turns to teacher evaluation, you will hear a chorus of groans. Teachers have a negative view toward the methods used to evaluate them for several reasons. First, our traditional methods of evaluating teachers use a one-size-fits-all approach. Teachers, on the other hand, know that teaching occurs in many different kinds of settings. Also, teachers think of current practices in teacher evaluation as something that is done to them, rather than something that they do for themselves. Reflecting on the meaning and evidence of good teaching in a particular setting is not encouraged when a principal reviews marks on a checklist or Likert scale type of form. For teachers to benefit from evaluation as a way of directing their professional growth, they need to play a more active role.

Teaching portfolios give teaching a context. The knowledge, skills, and values that teachers reveal are always in response to a unique set of circumstances. Who, what, why, and where they are teaching determines how they will teach. Teaching portfolios allow teachers to demonstrate what makes their teaching effective in their own environment.

Just as teaching portfolios let teachers define the context for their teaching, portfolios also allow teachers to accommodate diversity in the pupils they teach and encourage diversity in the ways that they teach. The actual evidence that teachers accumulate for inclusion in their teaching portfolios reveals much more about diversity of pupils and diversity of teaching styles than does a check mark by a principal.

The preparation of a teaching portfolio requires teachers to reflect on the meaning and evidence of effective teaching. When teachers have to explain to one another what they value in teaching and what they hope to accomplish as teachers, they are more likely to examine for themselves whether they are being effective. Self-knowledge is essential to self-change, and teaching portfolios empower teachers to change themselves by encouraging reflective thinking.

Teaching portfolios also facilitate professional dialogue among teachers. The use of mentors when preparing teaching portfolios encourages teachers to discuss much more than the materials that should be included. Conversations teachers have about teaching and about the best evidence of effective teaching for their particular situations give teachers the opportunity to engage one another in intellectual discussions about their profession.

Portfolios have a variety of uses for teacher assessment. Both beginning and experienced teachers stand to benefit. Portfolios help the beginning teacher identify strengths and plan a program for career development and provide the experienced teacher with impetus for professional rejuvenation. In both cases teaching portfolios are a means to integrate all the aspects of teaching so that teachers can see for themselves where they are and where they are going professionally.

REFERENCES

Berry, D. M., Kisch, J. A. Ryan, C. W. and Uphoff, J. K. (1991). *The process and product of portfolio construction.* Paper presented at the annual meeting of the American Educational Research Association, Chicago.

Biddle, J. R. and Lasley, T. J. (1991). *Portfolios and the process of teacher education.* Paper presented at the annual meeting of the American Educational Research Association, Chicago.

Bradley, A. (1994, April 20). Pioneers in professionalism. *Education Week,* 19–27.

Cole, D. J., Messner, P., Swonigan, H., and Tillman, B. (1991). *Portfolio structure and student profiles: An analysis of education student portfolio reflectivity scores.* Paper presented at the annual meeting of the American Educational Research Association, Chicago.

Green, J. E. and Smyser, S. O. (1995). Changing conceptions about teaching: A semantic differential study of teaching portfolios with pre-service teachers. *Teacher Education Quarterly, 22* (2), 43–53.

Richert, A. E. (1990). Teaching teachers to reflect: A consideration of program structure. *Journal of Curriculum Studies, 22,* 509–527.

Shulman, L. S. (1988). A union of insufficiencies: Strategies for teacher assessment in a period of educational reform. *Educational Leadership, 46* (3), 36–41.

Shulman, L. S. (1987). Knowledge and teaching: Foundations of the new reform. *Harvard Educational Review, 57* (1), 1–22.

Weinberger, H. and Didham, C. K. (1987). *Helping prospective teachers sell themselves: The portfolio as a marketing strategy.* Paper presented at the annual meeting of the Association of Teacher Educators, Houston.

CHAPTER 2

How Do You Begin a Teaching Portfolio?

OVERVIEW

A teaching portfolio is a *process* more than it is a *product*. The personal reflection and professional dialogue that occur during the preparation of a teaching portfolio are vital to the outcome. Moreover, the ongoing revision of the portfolio represents the habit of personal assessment that great teachers possess.

When beginning a teaching portfolio a teacher should pair off with a mentor, preferably one who has experience with portfolio preparation. The team should avoid a prescriptive approach to a teaching portfolio's organization and contents. The purpose of the portfolio's format is to fit the teacher and the teacher should not try to fit a rigid format. However, a point of departure is always helpful, and the five *I*'s – introduction, influences, instruction, individualization, and integration – are useful guidelines for planning a personalized portfolio.

ORGANIZING PRINCIPLES

When planning a teaching portfolio, a teacher should

- establish the purpose of the portfolio
- think reflectively on the evidence of good teaching
- use a peer mentor
- avoid a prescriptive approach to format or contents

- start with the five *I*'s
- establish a time line
- consider the portfolio a work in progress

MEET THREE TEACHERS WHO WILL DEVELOP TEACHING PORTFOLIOS

We have no rulebook or manual of regulations for developing portfolios. Therefore, when school districts or state departments of education try to dictate a uniform method of compiling one, they often miss the whole point. Developing a teaching portfolio is a process that should cause teachers to think about what they are doing, discuss with other teachers and administrators what they are doing, and describe to other teachers and administrators what they are doing.

Of course, if there are no rules or regulations on how to develop a teaching portfolio, then an essential question arises: How do you do it? The answer is obvious to teachers. You watch people who are developing their own portfolios. And, even though you realize that your teaching portfolio will not look exactly like someone else's, you can get a good idea of how to start yourself. Throughout this book you will get to know three teachers—each one at a different career phase and each one a different kind of teacher. Meet each one and observe them as they start to plan and create their own teaching portfolios.

Carmen Garcia's Teaching Portfolio

Carmen Garcia has been teaching for twenty-six years, and everyone agrees she is good at it. Her students love her, her students' parents love her, and her principal generally ends up shepherding new teachers past her door in the hope that they will learn something from her. Carmen, herself, knows she is a good teacher. She can't remember when she decided she had a knack for teaching, but it might have been in the fourth grade when she began to teach her younger brother how to read. In any event, teaching is something she has been doing well for a long time.

Carmen's room is a wonder to behold. Happiness and activity are everywhere, and Carmen keeps everything moving along with the skill of a conductor leading a highly energetic orchestra. She has learning centers in the corners, small groups working on the rug, independent readers in the bean-bag chair, and mold growing on the science table. Visitors to her room shake their heads at the effortless, serene way in which Carmen manages this chaos. They leave her room tired but happy after their brush with elementary education. Her students leave her room tired but happy each day, too.

Carmen has seen many changes in her twenty-six years in the classroom. One of the most notable is the change in her student population. When she first began teaching, nearly all her students were English speakers. But in the last ten or fifteen years her facility with Spanish has meant she has been assigned either to classes in which the students spoke only Spanish or to bilingual classrooms of English and Spanish speakers. She is happy to be able to move so freely to different types of classrooms, for, if the truth were known, the thing that worries Carmen the most about teaching is falling into a rut. She is an eager learner, always attending workshops on new educational techniques, and the idea that she could stop growing as a teacher worries her more and more as her years in the classroom increase. She has kept her enthusiasm for teaching by changing grades and schools frequently throughout the years, but now she wonders if her changes have merely put new names on the old material. She's beginning to think there might not be anything new in education that can excite her.

Carmen's principal would like to help her overcome her sense of boredom. He recognizes Carmen's talents and wishes she would be more free in sharing them with her peers. His efforts to encourage Carmen to take on more leadership roles have been rebuffed; she is not interested in committee work and says serving as a mentor to a peer feels too much like bragging. Carmen finds excuses for not carrying through her principal's suggestions. Her principal would like to change this situation, but Carmen is really so good in the classroom that her disinterest in mentoring seems like a very minor point. Her principal has bigger things to worry about—Marianne for one.

Marianne Miller's Teaching Portfolio

Marianne has been teaching first grade in Franklin Elementary School for only two years, but she taught first grade in another state for eleven years before her husband was transferred. As an experienced teacher, Marianne had expected to move easily into her new first-grade classroom, but things have been rocky from the start. Both Marianne and her principal know that this year is pivotal for Marianne. At the end of this year she will either receive or be denied tenure. Marianne blames her principal completely for all her difficulties. In her old school, she hadn't had to put up with any criticism.

Marianne blames her husband's transfer for the whole mess. She had been perfectly happy in her previous school; she had known the curriculum, had the whole year planned in advance, and had every bulletin board ready to go. Teaching in a new school had been just like starting over. The books and units were unfamiliar, none of her bulletin board borders fit, and this new group of first graders wasn't nearly as prepared as her old one. Marianne had not been too impressed with either the kindergarten teacher or the parents she had met.

Marianne had tried to make do as best she could. She had requisitioned blackline master books to fit the new curriculum, and she had purchased new bulletin board border material. As for her pupils, she was doing what she could to whip them into shape. She found extra worksheets for them, and she was trying to impress on them the value of hard work. No one seemed to appreciate any of this in the least, and Marianne was thoroughly discouraged at how little her efforts were valued.

It's hard for Marianne's principal to help her improve, because Marianne cannot seem to recognize any of her problems, and they are subtle enough to make them difficult to articulate. She is lazy and does the absolute minimum in her classroom, yet she follows the approved curriculum and completes all the books she is issued. Her class seems a little too subdued, and there are parent complaints about her extremely strict discipline; still, no one would be able to check "poor discipline" on the district evaluation checklist. She seems to have no instinctive or theoretical background that would help her improve her lessons, yet she has meticulously followed each specific suggestion given to her by her principal. The most worrisome thing that Marianne's principal can say about her teaching is that when he is in her classroom, he wants to get out. But there isn't a space on the district form for that comment either.

Gary Donovan's Teaching Portfolio

Gary began his first year of teaching at Emerson High School the way he had begun everything else he attempted. He jumped in with boundless energy and contagious enthusiasm. When he found out that he was going to teach both tech prep and college prep English classes, he said, "Great! I'll like the change of pace during the day." Of course, he knew that the two courses—both of them eleventh grade—were going to present special challenges for a beginning teacher. The tech prep classes would require lots of preparation; the new program did not use a textbook and depended heavily upon cooperative learning strategies and applications of computer technology. Also, the required reading list of the college prep course in American literature was enough to keep him busy full time. Still, Gary was fired up. His tech prep classes were going to teem with relevance, and his American lit classes were going to inspire a generation.

Gary's principal, Dr. McIntyre, knew she had found a go-getter when they first met. His strong academic record and his athletic background stood out among the other final candidates for the opening. But what most impressed Dr. McIntyre was Gary's success in student teaching. His supervising teacher called him the "best one to come along in years," and his recommendations consistently cited his eagerness to try innovative teaching strategies. Even though he was going to be stretched to the limits with his teaching schedule and coaching, Dr. McIntyre was pretty sure that Gary was not going to gravitate to the textbook-workbook, machine-scored-test mentality of so many of her other teachers.

Gary did not disappoint Dr. McIntyre. He immediately teamed up with a science teacher in the tech prep program, and together they planned and began a unit on bar coding. The science teacher, Monte Chandler, had the students that he and Gary shared learning the principles of physics by constructing a simple bar-code scanner and connecting it to a computer. Gary planned several communications projects around the bar-coding idea. He had one group responsible for planning, scripting, and producing a training video to teach new clerks how to use a bar-code device. Another group had to prepare a complete sales presentation that would persuade a store manager to invest in bar-coding technology. A third group had to write a technical manual for the computer software that went with the bar coder that Monte Chandler's class was making.

Gary started his college prep classes no less ambitiously. Instead of using the chronological approach that his textbook suggested, he began with a unit on genealogy. Students were going to interview their families, use a computer program to chart their ancestries, and write narrative accounts of their family histories. Then, he was going to set up reading stations in his classroom organized around the different cultures that the genealogies from his class included. There would be novels, short stories, folklore and ballads, chronicles from old magazines and newspapers, and diaries. He planned for the whole range of literary types to tie in to the students' personal histories. Putting together the bibliographies for each of the reading stations (there were fourteen) was consuming nearly all his time.

Of course, early in the year Gary learned that not all of his students were as eager to learn as he was to teach. All the group work that he had planned for his tech prep classes was letting some students slide by without making much of a contribution. Even more vexing was deciding how to grade the group projects.

Gary was overwhelmed. A few students were beginning to take advantage of his unstructured approach to classroom management, and wrestling practice started in two weeks. Now Dr. McIntyre was suggesting he do some kind of teaching portfolio as part of his beginning-teacher assistance program.

PLANNING THE PORTFOLIO

Since a portfolio is so personal and so self-directed, there are countless ways in which one can be organized. Some authors advocate organizing the portfolio around categories developed by Shulman, Haertel, and Bird (1988). These include: professional responsibilities, command of subject matter, content-specific and student-specific practices, and classroom management. Vavrus and Collins (1991) had good success with a portfolio organized around aspects of teaching that could be integrated with work in a teacher assessment center.

Several states and school districts have adopted the use of highly prescriptive portfolios in which a large number of items are required (Furtwengler, 1986; Terry and Eade, 1983). However, when state or school district policies prescribe a rigid format for a portfolio the main purpose is often obscured in the bureaucracy.

Other formats (Richert, 1990) are almost totally self-determined with the inclusion of nearly all items left to the teacher's discretion.

Wolf (1991) advocated a middle ground between the totally prescribed portfolio and the completely discretionary portfolio. The portfolio organization we described appears to be prescriptive in terms of format. Each portfolio contains the same five sections and expects a degree of teacher reflection. However, the specific items each teacher chooses to include are completely self-selected. We suggest documents that might prove useful in each section, but no specific items are required. Moreover, other methods for organizing a portfolio could be followed by a teacher. The very acts of choosing what to put in a portfolio and deciding how to organize it are useful, because they encourage teachers to reflect about teaching.

ESTABLISH THE PURPOSE OF THE PORTFOLIO

The first step in preparing a teaching portfolio is to establish its purpose. Teachers in various stages of their careers will all have different reasons for presenting evidence of their teaching skills. The most popular types of teaching portfolios are *the employment portfolio, the evaluation portfolio,* and *the professional development portfolio.* Although these several types of portfolios serve different purposes, they also overlap.

The Employment Portfolio

The employment portfolio presents the qualifications of a teacher who is applying for a position. In other words, the teacher is showcasing her or his strengths in a convincing manner—a manner that will persuade a school administrator to hire that teacher. Consequently, employment portfolios present a teacher's best work, and they are planned to reveal a teacher's full range of teaching skills to a prospective employer. When a teacher is developing an employment portfolio, one question stands out: How can I best present my teaching experience and skills to this particular school?

The Evaluation Portfolio

The evaluation portfolio is an outgrowth of the employment portfolio. In an evaluation portfolio the teacher is being evaluated in conjunction with career advancement. An evaluation portfolio may be used as part of a beginning-teacher assistance program or may be part of the process for evaluation for tenure or an annual review.

Evaluation portfolios are usually more prescriptive than employment portfolios. State departments or school districts outline specific aspects of teaching that need to be included so that the evaluator can look at uniform criteria. Of course, when teaching portfolios are used in conjunction with personnel decisions, rubrics for evaluation must be agreed upon ahead of time.

Evaluation portfolios can also be used by teachers for professional development. Both the beginning teacher and the teacher with several years of experience need to plan long range programs for professional growth. The evaluation portfolio almost always includes a section that describes areas in which the teacher wants to focus, and it will explain some of the professional development activities that the teacher will pursue.

The Professional Development Portfolio

For the veteran teacher, portfolios take on a vastly different character. The teacher has a job, and the teacher is established—probably even tenured. Therefore, the professional development portfolio is more of a strategy for invigorating the teacher's perspective on teaching. It is a self-examination that is intended to renew or sustain professional growth.

The sole purpose of a professional development portfolio is self-evaluation. Certainly other purposes can be identified, but the real reason an established teacher prepares a teaching portfolio is to reflect on the meaning of good teaching and engage in self-improvement. As a result, teachers preparing professional development portfolios should be encouraged to follow a flexible outline. Teachers must have the freedom to structure their portfolios in a way that suits their individual situations and personal preferences.

REFLECTION IS THE KEY

The professional development of a teacher is essentially a process of personal change, and personal change is essentially an interior process.

It is something that the teacher has to initiate and guide. It is not something that can be done to a teacher. Self-reflection, therefore, is the starting point for professional development. Naturally, it is the starting point for teaching portfolios as well.

Regardless of how a teacher organizes a teaching portfolio, reflective statements should be included. Most teaching portfolios will have several distinct sections—one for personal information, one for classroom teaching effectiveness, and perhaps another for a professional development plan. The formats may vary according to a teacher's purpose. Whatever the sections may be, each one should include a brief reflective statement—a short essay, we can call it—that explains why the teacher chose to include particular items in that section. The inclusion of the reflective statement causes the teacher to consider how or why a certain item reveals teaching effectiveness. Thinking through what to include and what not to include and justifying the choices in a few concise paragraphs forces a teacher to consider what is effective teaching and whether the teacher has any evidence to document effective teaching.

USE A PEER MENTOR

An irony in teaching is that it is a lonely profession. Even though teachers are surrounded by other people all day long, they rarely have the chance to form mentoring relationships with other teachers that can enrich and direct their professional growth.

Many states have successfully used mentoring as a way of guiding the development of first-year teachers. Ultimately, of course, the programs are only as good as the sincerity and skill of the mentors. But, we can conclude that first-year teachers are helped immensely by having peers to mentor them. One question remains, however: Why do we stop after one year?

Any teacher who seeks to grow professionally can benefit from a peer mentor. The process of preparing a teaching portfolio is ideally suited to forming and fostering peer mentoring among all teachers, even the veterans. The peer mentor adds another, nonthreatening perspective that is so often needed when a teacher begins to consider what is working and what is not working in the classroom.

The entire process of preparing a teaching portfolio should be undertaken with a peer mentor. The peer mentor should have frequent conversations with the teacher and offer advice on the portfolio's organization and contents. As a result, professional dialogue that is crucial to professional development occurs.

AVOID A PRESCRIPTIVE APPROACH

Portfolios are useful for assisting teachers in evaluating themselves because they avoid a prescriptive approach. The opportunity to tailor a format to suit individuals is the advantage that portfolios have over traditional methods of teacher evaluation. Teachers should consider their own teaching situations, their own teaching styles, and their own teaching strengths when they plan how to organize their portfolios.

Even though a prescriptive approach should be avoided, we can all benefit from some guidelines. Teachers should be given a flexible framework to use to begin planning a portfolio. However, they should be assured that they can modify the format if another organization better conveys the information they are trying to present.

THE FIVE *I*'S

We all like to have a road map when we start a trip. Of course, we might take different routes because we have different reasons for taking the trip. Even so, a recommended route helps in planning the journey. Similarly, a recommended structure can help many teachers plan their portfolios for the first time.

The Stanford Teacher Assessment Project developed prototypes for portfolios that included specific scenario areas (Vavrus and Collins, 1991). In the case of elementary literacy, the specific areas included assessment of students, planning and conducting integrated language arts instruction, and creating a literate environment. The four areas identified in biology were planning and preparation, instruction, evaluation and reflection, and professional exchange. Both the elementary literacy and the biology prototype portfolios included a background section as well. This method of organization proved effective when the teaching portfolio process was field tested (Vavrus and Collins, 1991).

Other methods for organizing a teaching portfolio exist, but the one that is recommended in this book was developed by Smyser and Green (1994). It is easily remembered as the five *I*'s format that includes the following sections: Introduction, Influences, Instruction, Individualization, and Integration.

Introduction

In the Introduction, the teacher provides background information on herself or himself, as well as on the school, and includes previous professional experience related to teaching and autobiographical information that highlights other experience with children. Typical contents are a resumé, a brief autobiography, and a short explanation of the school and classroom or teaching assignment. Some teachers outline their philosophy of education in this section.

Influences

The Influences section captures the richness of the classroom environment that the teacher creates. Room arrangements and displays that are an outgrowth of the curriculum are documented in this section. Depending upon the grade level or subject, the actual items that a teacher includes vary.

Reflective statements are prominent in the Influences section. Without brief explanations of why certain items are included and brief notes explaining the importance of each item, the Influences section runs the risk of becoming little more than a photo album or scrapbook.

Instruction

The Instruction section is devoted to the actual teaching—both the planning and the delivery of instruction. Unit plans and lesson plans that are the personal work of the teacher, laboratory activities, and various instructional aids that the teacher has constructed are typical items. Again, the reflective statement is vital. It is only when the teacher explains what is really important in teaching and presents evidence that those professional values are revealed in the classroom that someone else can begin to judge whether that teacher is effective.

Individualization

In the Individualization section the teacher conveys how individual needs of the students are being met. Here the teacher includes examples of teacher-designed student assessment tools. These might include informal reading inventories, unit tests, or IEPs. In addition, this section contains examples of how the teacher accommodates the special needs of children.

Integration

The Integration section ties the whole portfolio together and may include other forms of evaluation, such as a principal's evaluation of a lesson. Some teachers will place their philosophy of education here instead of at the beginning, reasoning that it is in this section that the teacher can be judged in terms of the material presented in the previous sections. Without question, the most crucial entry in the Integration section is the professional development plan in which the teacher sets out professional goals and explains a strategy for reaching them.

SET A TIME LINE

One can clearly see that developing a teaching portfolio is a difficult and time-consuming process. It certainly is one that cannot be hurried. The best approach is to plan a year-long process. Teachers need to give all their attention to their classroom teaching duties, and they have little energy or time for special projects. Spreading the process of preparing the portfolio over the span of a year serves two purposes. First, the teacher can work on the portfolio at a leisurely pace that allows for the personal reflection and dialogue with a peer mentor that are so vital for the process to be beneficial. Also, the relaxed schedule does not encroach on the teacher's primary duties.

Allowing a couple of months for some in-service training sessions on the portfolio process and about a month to write each section, a portfolio project that begins in September can usually be completed by the following April. The last chapter recommends a more detailed schedule for completing a portfolio.

A TEACHING PORTFOLIO IS A WORK IN PROGRESS

If you agree that the professional growth of a teacher is a continuing process, then you need to view the teaching portfolio as a work in progress. First of all, the type of portfolio that one keeps will change as a teacher's career develops. A teaching portfolio started as part of a preservice teacher education program is revised after student teaching into an employment portfolio. The employment portfolio changes into an evaluation portfolio during the teacher's first several years. Then, after the teacher is established as an experienced teacher, the evaluation portfolio evolves into a professional development portfolio. As a teacher's professional assignments change or as professional goals change, the professional development portfolio becomes the stimulus for focusing and directing the teacher's professional growth. All the while, from the point at which the portfolio begins in preservice teacher education to its evolution into a professional development portfolio, the main ingredients in the process are present. The teacher is self-reflecting, engaging in professional dialogue on the meaning of good teaching, and presenting evidence of good teaching.

SUMMARY

A teaching portfolio can serve several purposes. It can help a beginning teacher who is seeking employment showcase teaching experience, present evidence of teaching effectiveness as part of an evaluation process, or be used for professional development.

Regardless of the purpose, a portfolio must be viewed as an ongoing process. Self-reflection and professional dialogue are the cornerstones.

The format that a portfolio takes should not be prescribed. A teacher's specific teaching situation and individual professional needs are the factors that should determine how a portfolio is organized. However, guidelines are helpful. The five *I*'s — introduction, influences, instruction, individualization, and integration — are suggested as the way to begin planning.

REFERENCES

Furtwengler, Carol. (1986). *Multiple data sources in teacher evaluation.* Paper presented at the National Council on Measurement in Education, San Francisco.

Richert, A. E. (1990). Teaching teachers to reflect: A consideration of program structure. *Journal of Curriculum Studies, 22,* 509–527.

Shulman, L., Haertel, E., and Bird, T. (1988). *Toward alternative assessments of* teaching: A report of work in progress. Unpublished manuscripts, Stanford University.

Smyser, S. O. and Green, J. E. (1994). Teaching portfolios: Applications for teacher education. *Ohio-Michigan Journal of Teacher Education, 8* (1), 47-54.

Terry, Gwenith L. and Eade, Gordon E. (1983). *The portfolio process: New roles for meeting challenges in professional development.* Paper presented at the annual meeting of the Association of Teacher Educators, Pensacola, FL.

Vavrus, L. G. and Collins, A. (1991). Portfolio documentation and assessment center exercises: A marriage made for teacher assessment. *Teacher Education Quarterly, 18* (3), 13-29.

Wolf, K. (1991). The school teacher's portfolio: Issues in design, implementation and evaluation. *Phi Delta Kappan, 73,* (2), 129-136.

CHAPTER 3

Portfolio Development: The Introduction Section

OVERVIEW

EXCELLENT teachers understand that the ways they choose to present the concepts of their disciplines depend on their own backgrounds and philosophies, the specific content involved, and the needs of the student. It is the match between the student's needs and the teacher's methods that produces learning, and it is impossible to assess skillful teaching apart from its content and context.

The Introduction section of the five-section portfolio provides the opportunity to introduce both the teacher's background and the teaching situation. Background information about the teacher belongs in this section. Descriptions of the students, school, and general teaching environment set the stage for the evaluation of the teaching that takes place.

ORGANIZING PRINCIPLES

- Three teachers begin their portfolios.
- The Introduction section should include entries to describe the teacher, the student, the content, and the school.
- Reflection upon these entries should focus on how they impact the teacher.

PLANNING THE INTRODUCTION SECTION

Carmen Garcia's Introduction Section

Carmen embraced the idea of a teaching portfolio with uncharacteristic enthusiasm when she was approached by her principal. She had seen fads come and go, and she had grown used to ignoring most of them. This portfolio idea, though, fit in beautifully with her view of teaching. Hadn't she been saying for years that her teaching couldn't possibly be evaluated on the basis of two brief visits a year by her principal? Hadn't she complained repeatedly that nothing in the currently used evaluation process helped her to become a better teacher? At last, here was an opportunity for her to examine her own teaching, set some personally valuable goals, and do all of this with the help of a colleague.

Carmen went home from the district in-service meeting, at which portfolios had been introduced, bursting with excitement. She immediately sat down at her desk to start her Introduction, and this is where her troubles began. As Carmen sat at her desk considering her long career in teaching, the enormity of the portfolio task began to set in. How could she summarize twenty-six years of teaching? Deciding what was important enough to put in and what should be left out seemed to be a nearly impossible chore. And she wasn't sure she could find the words to describe the rare blend of science and art that made her teaching powerful.

In an effort to compose her thoughts, Carmen took out the guidelines sheet she had received. Reasoning that it was a good idea to begin at the beginning, she reviewed the five sections of the portfolio and then turned her attention to the Introduction section. This proved almost no help in calming her fears. The district guidelines suggested such items as a resumé and an autobiography. Well, Carmen hadn't needed a resumé for at least fifteen years. She wasn't even sure she could find the one she had used last. An autobiography of just her years in teaching could run to novel length. How on earth to begin? Carmen decided to call her portfolio partner. Surely Emily had faced these same problems when she had begun her own portfolio.

Marianne Miller's Introduction Section

When Marianne came home from the district training sessions, she immediately filed the portfolio handouts in her to-look-at-someday file. That was six weeks ago, and suddenly she was being reminded by her principal that the first section should be completed by the end of the month. One more thing to do. Her principal suggested she submit a portfolio as part of her evaluation for tenure this year. Well, she wanted tenure and decided she better not rock the boat. Marianne retireved the handouts and tried to remember what had been said in the meeting.

Yes, here it all was. She was to prepare a five-section document. The first section was labeled Introduction, and there was a list of items that needed to be included. Better yet, she had been assigned someone at the school who would tell her how to do this. Her portfolio partner was John, a fourth-grade teacher. She knew who he was, of course, but since she was a primary teacher and he taught an intermediate grade, their schedules did not coincide. She decided to set up an after-school meeting with him as soon as possible so that she could get this portfolio chore out of the way.

The meeting proved a disappointment to Marianne. John kept asking her why she was including certain documents; he did not seem to think it was reason enough that the district office had suggested it. He wanted to know why she planned to include her state teaching credential, if her resumé was really necessary, and what the autobiography said about her teaching.

Marianne had gone to the meeting prepared to fulfill a prescriptive list of required documents. She had not planned to reflect upon what she thought should go into a teaching portfolio. She had not thought she would be expected to take responsibility for describing and evaluating her own teaching. Evaluation had always been something the principal had taken care of until now. Wasn't that what evaluation meant? And yet here was John asking these awkward questions.

When Marianne went home, a couple of John's final comments resonated. She remembered him saying, "Before you put anything into your portfolio, consider whether it describes you as a teacher." As she thought about that, she recalled the question he had urged her to ask herself: Is the teacher I am describing the kind of teacher I want to be?

Gary Donovan's Introduction Section

Gary wasn't eager to start his teaching portfolio. In September he attended the initial training sessions with his portfolio partner, a social studies teacher who had developed her teaching portfolio the previous year. He was beginning to see how much was involved. He already understood the process well enough to know that he would have to give the project some serious thought and considerable time. However, he liked the idea of his first year's teaching evaluations being linked to his special situation and some of the new approaches he was trying in his classroom. Mainly, his anxiety came from his uncertainty of where to begin and where to find the time. Had it not been for his portfolio partner, Allison Taylor, Gary knew he would have been totally lost. She was the one who told him to begin with an outline and go one step at a time. Gary and Allison decided to follow the recommended format and began brainstorming the kinds of things that he should include.

Of course, Gary first zeroed in to his particular reason for creating a teaching portfolio. As a beginning teacher, he was going to use the portfolio to showcase his strengths as a teacher so that he would be re-hired for the following year. Therefore, he wanted to find a way to point out the areas where he needed to set some professional goals.

After he and Allison came up with some ideas for the things he would place in his portfolio, they realized that the usual three-ring-binder format wasn't going to work. Instead, he decided to use an expanding file that would let him insert folders and large envelopes containing his exhibits. This way he could include a videotape of some segments from several of his classes, as well as examples of student work from his tech prep course.

Next, Gary and Allison turned their attention to the first section: the Introduction. Allison got Gary started by asking him one question: If someone has to make a bottom-line decision about whether to rehire you, what personal and professional data do you want them to have? That started them talking, and Allison jotted down Gary's ideas. Next, they looked over the list, organized it a little, added some new items, and scratched off a few. When they had finished their conversation, Gary's Introduction section had pretty well taken shape.

THE CONTENTS OF THE INTRODUCTION SECTION

Good teaching is a very holistic activity. It is both content specific and context embedded. Excellent teachers not only understand the content they teach, but also realize that they will need to use diverse methods to teach the content depending upon the needs of their students. It is, therefore, necessary that any document designed to assess teaching allows the display of these diverse methods. The five-section portfolio described in this book is one way, though admittedly not the only way of doing this.

The Introduction section is especially useful for setting the stage in which the individual teaches. By describing the courses or grade level taught and including information about any special expertise in specific areas, the teacher is able to display content knowledge. In addition to describing what is being taught, it is also necessary to describe who is being taught. This is the context in which the teacher intends to transfer the knowledge of the subject matter. The Introduction section is the place to detail the environment that frames the particular teacher's efforts to teach the content.

The Introduction section, then, generally contains entries designed to describe the teacher and to describe the teaching environment. Two very common entries used to help describe the teacher are the autobiography and the resumé.

Most teachers have never written an autobiography before, and they are surprised at the many events in their lives that have influenced their style and philosophy of teaching. The autobiography needs to be tightly focused, however, to be useful. A blow-by-blow account of the last forty years will do very little to explain how and why someone is the teacher he or she is today. This autobiography needs to emphasize events that helped shape the teacher.

The resumé is naturally more career directed than the autobiography, but it should also follow the guideline of describing the teacher. The reflection needed to decide what career activities to include on the resumé forces a teacher to ask what kind of a teacher he or she is describing.

In addition to documents that describe the teacher's backgound, the Introduction section may also include items that describe the teaching environment in which this teacher works. One of the benefits of portfolios is that they are able to capture the diverse situations in which teaching takes place. In order to truly understand why a teacher teaches in a certain way, it is important to understand the specific circumstances. Descriptions of the types of students in the classroom are important pieces of information. School description, pictures, mission statements, and student profiles also could be included here, as well as special features about the student body or the teacher's class. The reflective statements in this section should examine how a teacher's skills have been honed by past experiences and framed by the present situation. By looking at the portfolios of Carmen, Marianne, and Gary we can learn how these three teachers chose to fulfill the goals of the Introduction section.

THREE TEACHERS PLAN THE INTRODUCTION SECTION

Carmen's Introduction

Carmen's first difficulty, and it turned out to be a concern for her throughout the development of her portfolio, was how to select a few most important pieces of evidence from a multitude of productive years spent in the classroom. She decided to begin by updating her resumé. In doing this she found she not only needed to add things she had accomplished in the last decade, she also wanted to change the focus of the document. She was very proud of her habit of continuing to learn and improve as a teacher, so she included an entire section on workshops and classes she had attended. She was also very pleased with her work as a bilingual teacher, and she highlighted her experiences in this area both as a classroom teacher and as a community volunteer.

Next, Carmen decided to write her autobiography. This turned out to be a difficult but satisfying task. She was able to see and express how her experiences of being the eldest child in the family and the teacher of her younger siblings had helped her become an organized, if rather headstrong, teacher. She also saw how those early experiences had influenced her management style in the classroom. She had developed a gentle, soft-spoken technique that worked well with the younger children in her family, and she had continued to find success with this in her classroom. In writing her autobiography, Carmen ran across several examples of work she had done while she was an elementary student. While this seemed like a rather unusual entry for a teaching portfolio, she decided to include several items (see Figure 3.1). If a portfolio is to be a collection of authentic evidence describing a teacher, what better place to start than with the teacher as student she reasoned.

Finally, Carmen included several documents that introduced her teaching situation. She wrote short descriptions of the school and the students in her class. She added two pages from the *All about Me* book

hous   for   est   time   I

saw   snowe   at   my   ants

i   wen't   to   my   ants

Figure 3.1 Carmen's personal school work.

MEET ___WHITNEY___ G.___

1.   This is what I look like. I have blonde hair, blue eyes, and I'm 4'7. I wear size 5 in shoes.

2.   These are the people in my family. Mom, Dad, older Brother, and cat.

3.   The best thing about me is I'm kinda a good gymnast and a GREAT swimmer.

4.   My favorite part of school is History, P.E., Computers, and Reading.

I like it because they're all fun, and interesting.

5.   The best thing I like to do when I have free time is watch T.V. and talk on the phone.

6.   My favorite books are about summers.

7.   When I grow up I want to teach handicap kids gymnastics.

8.   If I could change one thing I would shelter and feed the homeless.

Figure 3.2 Carmen's sample getting acquainted page.

she had made with her students at the beginning of the year when they were getting to know each other (see Figure 3.2). A recent class photograph was Carmen's last entry in her Introduction section.

Gary's Introduction

After his conversation with Allison, Gary had listed the five documents he planned to include in the Introduction section.

- professional assignment
- professional resumé
- personal autobiography
- statement of philosophy of education
- teaching certificate

First, Gary wrote a one-page summary of his professional assignment at Emerson High School. He briefly described the classes he was teaching and gave some general information about his students. He also mentioned his coaching responsibilities. He used four subheadings to organize his thoughts: Emerson High School, Teaching Assignment, Student Characteristics, and Extracurricular Assignments.

Gary used the basic resumé format that he had used to apply for his job at Emerson. He replaced most of the entries about his college activities with his current professional activities, such as committee work and community service. After the resumé, Gary wrote a short autobiography. When he and Allison decided to include one, his first question was, "How long?" Allison answered, "You mean how short?" She stressed that the point of an autobiography in a teaching portfolio is to bring out those experiences that have influenced you as a teacher, but do not get revealed in a resumé. She said to imagine an interviewer saying, "Tell me about yourself," and then to answer the question in a minute or less. Her advice was to stick to events, people, and background that really made a difference in what kind of a teacher you are.

Gary then decided to break away from the recommended practice of placing his philosophy statement in the last section—the one on integration. (The idea is that the Integration section pulls everything together—your philosophy, your self-evaluation of your strengths and areas where you want to improve, and your long-term professional goals.) He thought it made more sense, however, to open the portfolio with a statement of his beliefs on learning and teaching. The only ad-

---

Credo on Teaching

I am a teacher. Period. I am not a teacher of English, or a teacher of history, or a teacher of this, or a teacher of that. Just simply, I am a teacher. I believe that the soul of a teacher is known not by subjects taught, but rather by students learning. I am compelled, therefore, to consider several questions which, if I ever answer them satisfactorily, shall form my credo on teaching.

What is a **teacher**?	A guide and companion on the journey of learning; and, therefore, a student.
What is a **student**?	A human being engaged in the process of **discovery**.
What is **discovery**?	Asking the right questions, using the right methods of inquiry, then questioning the answers to enable **learning**.
What is **learning**?	Activity of thought and human feeling directed toward the accomplishment of **goals**.
What are the **goals**?	**Liberated minds** and harmony in **community**.

I try to judge my success as a teacher by the extent to which these beliefs are reflected in my teaching.

Figure 3.3 Gary Donovan's teaching philosophy.

vice he got from Allison was to keep his philosophy statement to two pages or less and avoid jargon. As she said, "Try not to use a single word that ends in *ism*. Just explain your fundamental beliefs about the main purposes of formal education and connect that to how you think schools and teachers can best accomplish those purposes" (see Figure 3.3).

The last item that Gary included was a copy of his state teaching certificate. He thought it would be useful to document his additional credentials to teach at the middle school grade level and his additional certification to teach social studies.

Marianne's Introduction

Marianne also discovered in this very first section the concern she would grapple with throughout the development of her entire portfolio. She had a very difficult time finding any documents that were personal enough to describe her teaching accurately. Her Introduction section ended up containing only three items, and only one of those was very unique.

First, she put in the mission statement of Franklin School. This was the statement that everyone in the school was supposed to use as a guiding light for his or her teaching, and so she didn't see how she could go wrong with it.

Second, she included her teaching certificate. She was certified in two states, and she thought it meaningful that two state boards had deemed her worthy of a teaching license.

Finally, she added her resume. She already had a current resume — the one she had updated only two years ago when her husband had been transferred and she had needed to look for work.

When she had completed the Introduction section, she took it to John. Every single one of her entries was on the suggestion sheet from the district office, yet John did not seem too pleased. He seemed to have something more in mind.

John tried discretely to explain how impersonal and routine all of her items were. He also mentioned that she might have saved even these superficial documents by thoughtfully addressing what each item illustrated about her teaching in her reflective statement. Instead, her reflective statement read more like a table of contents with no evident introspection.

John also was concerned about Marianne's obvious lack of effort in beginning her portfolio. The in-service guidelines and his own attempts at motivation had apparently made little impact on Marianne. She still considered the portfolio an onerous task, and she was only doing one to pacify her principal. She was completing this task in as hurried and risk-free way as she knew how. John knew that unless Marianne was willing to invest more time, effort, and thought on her portfolio, it would never become a valuable tool for her. He just didn't know how to get her to agree.

SUMMARY

Sample Information Included	Sample Items Included
• Background information	• Autobiography • Personal school papers
• Professional experiences	• Resumé • Teaching credentials
• Philosophy of education	• Statement of beliefs on teaching and learning
• Present teaching situation	• Description of school • Description of students • Class photographs

CHAPTER 4

Portfolio Development: The Influences Section

OVERVIEW

MANY things can influence how well students learn the subject matter that is taught in a class, and many of these aspects do not relate directly to how well a lesson is presented. Excellent, well-conceived lessons may not result in learning for a variety of reasons.

The Influences section of the portfolio describes all of the peripheral, yet important, circumstances that affect learning. Some of these important influences include the physical environment in which teaching takes place, materials used to present or support the curriculum, and the motivation or discipline methods used in the classroom. The degree to which each of these aspects supports the philosophy and purpose of the teacher is the main question the Influences section seeks to answer.

ORGANIZING PRINCIPLES

- Three teachers develop their Influences sections.
- A rich learning environment influences success in teaching.
- The Influences section may include items that describe classroom environment, materials used, and discipline methods.
- Reflection focuses on how the teacher influences learning.

39

PLANNING THE INFLUENCES SECTION

Carmen Garcia's Influences Section

Walking into Carmen's classroom is like walking into a word factory that has exploded. Words are strewn about everywhere. They litter the walls and bulletin boards, they clutter every desk, and a great many of them are being spoken aloud by numerous students all at once. The effect is a little daunting, and visitors usually need a few minutes after entering the room before they can begin to make sense of it all. But there is a rather happily chaotic order to the room.

It is immediately apparent that Carmen believes in providing an environment that stimulates her fifth graders. One bulletin board is interactive and pertains to the students' recent study of weather patterns in North America. Another bulletin board has an ongoing time line to which the students add as they make their way through their state's history. Several bulletin boards are filled with student work, essays, poems, and reports about famous explorers. Every spare bit of wall space is papered with information, science stumpers, the word of the day, and rules for punctuation.

It isn't only the wall space that is stimulating; the counters and corners of the room are also filled with learning opportunities. There are several ongoing learning centers. A listening center features books on tape. The creative writing center contains ever-changing story starters and student work in various stages of the writing process. The science center currently displays a tornado in a bottle and other weather-related experiments. There is even a dress-up area in one corner. This last center is routinely criticized by visitors to the room, but Carmen keeps it because she strongly believes it strengthens her students' oral language development.

Oral language development is one of the key activities that keeps Carmen's room fairly noisy. She encourages her students to work together and to talk about their work. The desks in the room are arranged in pods of four. Carmen rearranges the pods frequently to give the students an opportunity to work with many types of learners. Many of Carmen's assignments specifically require the students to work together. This, of course, leads to many voices speaking at once, which means the room often operates at the low-roar noise level. When questioned about this, Carmen laughs comfortably and remarks that all the noise is productive noise. "Good noise," she calls it.

In fact, Carmen seems comfortable about her whole room. The noise, movement, and visual stimulation do not appear daunting to her in the least. At this moment she is seated comfortably on the floor with one pod of students who need some help with the skit they are writing about one of the state's early settlers. Carmen asks a few questions that help to focus the group, and then she moves easily to another pod to assess progress and offer suggestions. The products of these cooperative groups will eventually be displayed around the room, completing the cycle of a stimulating environment that produces learning that, in turn, produces a more stimulating environment.

Gary Donovan's Influences Section

By November Gary's room is teeming with ideas and activity. A paperback book library and several pieces of casual furniture are against the back wall. This day, as nearly always, a student is browsing through the collection. Posters, mostly the kind that depict landscapes or unique portraits with literary captions, decorate the area. A display of student writing from a unit on Transcendentalism is in a corner at the front of the room, and a photograph of the student in early nineteenth-century costume is next to each writing exhibit. Some of the exhibits are journals of Walden-like experiences, and others are free-verse poems. One student wrote an antislavery song and illustrated the manuscript with original pencil drawings of men and women in chains. The display is incomplete, however, and some of the photographs have been defaced.

During this visit Gary is in the middle of his tech prep class. He is working with a group of eight students around a cluster of four computers. Gary is helping several students with a desktop-publishing project. The students have designed a personnel application form, and they are in the process of laying it out in a four-page-leaflet format. While the students he is helping are intent, the others do not seem to be making the same progress.

Across the room a group of ten students, divided into pairs, are engaged in an employment-interviewing simulation. A couple of the pairs are on task and proceeding in very businesslike fashion; however, the other teams are excitedly chatting about their personal affairs. One student is doing homework for another class, and one is sleeping.

About halfway through the period Gary looks up from the desktop-publishing project and tells the students in the interviewing simulation to finish the interviews; he then gives them instructions for writing their critiques. The interviewers are to complete a critique form that a guest personnel director had previously explained to the students. The interviewees were to complete their own self-evaluations using the same form. All the students in the simulation went to work, and Gary turned his attention back to the group at the computer cluster.

Gary's room has the appearance of dishevelment with a purpose. Desks are in no particular configuration, except for the pairs of students participating in the simulation. The overall effect of the room is one of a lot of unfinished business.

One interesting feature is a communications device that Gary arranged in order to stay in touch with parents. He uses the computer modem's telephone line to receive voice mail from parents. A parent can call and leave a message asking for a progress report. The students know how to retrieve their individual test and assignment scores from Gary's electronic gradebook and can print the corresponding report, complete with Gary's latest comments, to take home. Of course, Gary requires students to return the report with a parent's signature.

Gary is pleased with the system because it has stimulated parent interest and gets students to use the technology as well as monitor their own progress.

Marianne Miller's Influences Section

Marianne's first-grade classroom resembles both Gary's and Carmen's in a number of ways. The parallels with Carmen's fifth grade are immediately noticeable. Marianne's bulletin boards are all filled with colorful figures. One board has a birthday chart that stays up all year. Another has professionally produced animal characters listing the rules of good citizenship in the classroom. This board remains throughout the year, too. The third display area has a picture of a large tiger congratulating students for their good work. The papers displayed this month are all of the 100-percent spelling tests. The 100-percent science tests are already stacked and ready to display when the bulletin board is changed next month.

Marianne's strength is orderliness, and this trait can be seen around her classroom. Her students' desks are arranged in rows, and students generally work quietly at their own desks. Marianne believes children, especially first graders, benefit from a quiet, structured environment. She, therefore, does not approve of the constant activity and chatter of Carmen's classroom. She also does not appreciate the cooperative group work that Gary uses so well. Her classroom is uncluttered, and as the teacher, she directs each lesson. The atmosphere in Marianne's room is one of containment, with all the children bending silently over the papers at their individual desks. Discipline is very important to Marianne, and she is proud of her reputation as a disciplinarian. Her classroom rules are posted and were thoroughly discussed at the beginning of the year. Each broken rule carries a penalty ranging from a warning to a trip to the office, and these punishments are also posted. Marianne enforces these rules consistently, and she has found that she is rarely challenged after the first couple of weeks of school.

Yes, at first glance, Marianne's room resembles the excellent learning environments constructed by Carmen and Gary. However, upon closer scrutiny, it is obvious that Marianne's desire for orderliness has resulted in a rather sterile room. There are no extra books or resources around the room. The majority of the vast number of papers the students complete are never displayed. And, she thinks learning centers would only add clutter.

The regimentation of the room, while initially appearing to be good discipline, means that students have very little opportunity to practice their oral language. In fact, they rarely even ask a question. Marianne values quiet and students never work together. Besides, Marianne feels that the projects that are often the product of group work would just add mess to the room.

Marianne's colorful room seems inviting. However, there are signs everywhere of Marianne's reluctance to do more than is absolutely necessary or to undertake the work involved in any changes. The bulletin boards are purchased and rarely changed. They do not connect to or support the curriculum in any way. The computer in the back of the classroom is never plugged in. None of this worries Marianne in the least. She is comfortable and complacent in this atmosphere in which

she has been teaching for the last thirteen years and sees nothing that
needs to be improved.

INFLUENCES: WHAT MAKES YOUR CLASSROOM
THE WAY IT IS

The Influences section of the portfolio is designed to capture all the
many areas that influence the act of teaching and to do so in a way that
highlights strengths and pinpoints weaknesses. The influences can be
many and varied and might include the room decor, room arrangement, and use of learning centers. The general ambiance or working
atmosphere can be detailed in this section. This often translates as a
discipline philosophy or plan. Materials the teacher has collected, specialized bibliographies that he or she has prepared, and technology the
teacher uses to support learning should be included.

Various studies have found that the richness of the environment in
which a student is placed will have a strong influence on how well the
student learns. In addition, in his landmark synthesis of numerous
studies dealing with change in human characteristics, Bloom (1964)
reports that not only is environment important but also that it plays an
even stronger role if the student is at a stage of rapid growth. Though
we know environment influences teaching, it is rarely treated in anything more than a very superficial way in the evaluation of teaching. If
it is addressed at all, it is only to check yes beside the checklist entry
"provides an environment conducive to learning." Or perhaps it is noted
in an incidental remark in the comment section of an evaluation such
as, "Your room looks very nice." Neither of these cursory remarks will
be very helpful in assisting teachers in identifying the positive attributes of their classroom environments and in improving the less positive aspects.

The Influences section of the portfolio often contains several articles
to illustrate outside influences upon teaching and photographs of particularly effective bulletin boards and learning centers. Diagrams of room
arrangements or plans for flexible groupings belong in this section.
Bibliographies teachers have prepared to augment their teaching can be
included, as can learning games, manipulatives, card files or other
teacher-made materials that enhance the learning environment. Lists of
software or ways in which teachers use technology are also appropriate
inclusions.

One of the real strengths of portfolios is that they are personalized to a teacher's style, grade level, and subject matter. The fact that a first-grade classroom environment cannot and should not be identical to a high school English class does not present difficulty in the development of a portfolio. In fact, each teacher at each level should be able to include evidence of an appropriate learning environment and also areas in which that environment can be improved. Every article included needs to be thought about carefully in terms of what it says about the teacher. Every picture and diagram must be labeled to explain what it shows and why this is important. The reflective statement in this section should examine the teacher's philosophy and whether the environment supports that philosophy. A critical look at self-improvement should be part of the reflective statement. Let's examine how our three teachers accomplish this task.

THREE TEACHERS PLAN THE INFLUENCES SECTION

Carmen Describes How Her Classroom Influences Learning

Carmen, an experienced and creative teacher, has structured a learning environment of which she can be proud. Her classroom reflects her philosophy and zeal for teaching in many ways. First, she believes in a visually stimulating classroom with an emphasis on literacy. Her portfolio includes photographs of several of her favorite bulletin boards. She was particularly proud of the interactive bulletin boards that are directly related to the curriculum or were products of student work.

Carmen also believes in a student-centered, active classroom. Her room arrangement with pods and learning centers reflects this belief, and her portfolio includes a diagram of her room arrangement (see Figure 4.1), her schedule that details time for working in groups, and a picture of a group working together.

Finally Carmen emphasizes curriculum integration in her classroom and makes sure her environment supports that. Each year she lists her major content topics, how the learning centers will support these, and which bulletin boards to use with each topic. She decided to include her planning document that showed how she arranged her classroom to follow her yearly curriculum (see Figure 4.2).

Even though Carmen has a wonderful classroom environment, de-

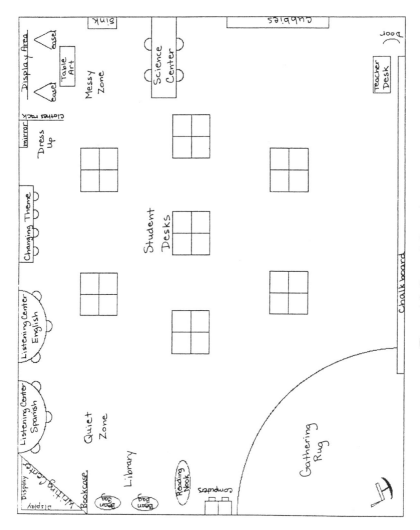

Figure 4.1 Carmen's floor plan.

	September	October	November	December	January
Theme	Survival	Freedom	Native Americans	Native Americans	Civil War
Language Arts	Witch of Blackbird Pond, sentence structure	Ben Hte, Johnny Tremain, contractions, nouns, verbs	Island of the Blue Dolphins, details, adverbs	Sign of the Beaver, summarization, pronouns	Slave Dancer Across Five April, Prefixes, suffixes
Social Studies	U.S. Colonization	U.S. War of Independence, Constitution	Native Americans	Native Americans	Civil War
Science	Natural resources as aids to colonization	Water Cycle	landforms	food chain	light + sound
Math	Review of Arithmetic operation	Estimating, 3 digit multiplic.	2 digit divisors	3 digit divisors	Geometry: Area, volume
Misc	Foods of Colonists	Music of Independence War	Native American artwork	Native American instruments + music	Music of Civil War

	February	March	April	May	June
Theme	Folk Heroes	Heroes Today	Responsibility	Space	Space
Language Arts	Tall tales, Adj; Plot, setting, Writing Tall tales	Biographies, Fact/Opinion, Writing autobio.	Number the Stars, letter writing, reference books	Wrinkle in Time, outlining, report writing	Swiftly Tilting Planet, report writing
Social Studies	U.S. Industrialization	Peoples of the U.S.	U.S. government	U.S. economics	U.S. Today
Science	Machines - Simple, compound, Friction	Weather/Climate as they influence settlement	Energy - Alternative sources	Astronomy	Space exploration
Math	Fractions - Lowest common denominator	Fractions - Operations	Decimals: +,-,x	Money; +,-,x,÷	Geometry
Misc	Dramatization of tall tale	Career Day - Parent Volunteers	Mock election	Solar Art	Field trip - Solarium

Figure 4.2 Carmen's yearly planning document.

veloping this section of the portfolio helped her to notice an area in which she could improve. As she tried to decide what to include, it became apparent that her room was stimulating almost to the point of overstimulation for some students. She had so many pictures, diagrams, and lists that it seemed impossible to select only a few. She began to see why some children were overwhelmed by her room. This especially seemed true of children who preferred to work alone or those who needed quiet in order to work. In her reflective statement, Carmen established the goals of finding a way to carve out a quiet space in her environment and adding a little more independent work to her schedule.

Gary Looks at How His Classroom Influences Learning

Gary, as a first year teacher, was not aware of the significant strides he had already made in structuring a rich environment. He felt he had much to improve in this area. However, as he searched for evidence to include in his portfolio, he was happy to note three strengths.

First, the bulletin boards and displays he did have were well thought out and supported his curriculum. He included several pictures of these and resolved to do more of them.

Second, Gary has a wonderful knowledge of his subject matter. This knowledge means that he has developed several specialized bibliographies, and he included one.

Finally, Gary's knowledge of ways to use computers to enhance the study of language and literature strengthens his teaching. He decided to include a representative bibliography of effective software, as well as an overview of the ways he used technology in his classroom throughout the year.

Gary was pleasantly surprised that his classroom environment was more stimulating than he had thought. However, the portfolio helped him to realize that he needed more displays and that his use of technology needed to be more intentional and organized. These were the goals he included in his reflective statement.

Figure 4.3 lists the exhibits that Gary decided to include in his Influences section.

Marianne Finds That Inventing Exhibits Is Difficult

Marianne had the opposite problem from Carmen with this section of the portfolio. While Carmen had so many articles she found it hard

Sample Items from Gary's *Influences* Section

Photo of students using the classroom library

Bulletin board of student writing samples

Bulletin board of "Transcendental Authors"

Annotated bibliography of computer software used in classroom management

Floor plan of Tech Prep classroom

Sample letters to parents in conjunction with classroom management plan

Figure 4.3.

to be selective, Marianne had a hard time coming up with anything to put into this section. The guidelines for the Influences section listed photographs of bulletin boards, diagrams of room arrangements, and bibliographies of selected materials as suggestions, but none of these seemed to work for her. Her bulletin boards were all store-bought, and it seemed silly to take a picture of them. Her room arrangement was simply desks in rows, which hardly seemed worthy of a drawing. Luckily, she had a strong, consistent discipline policy that was all ready to go, or she would have found nothing to put in this section.

In the end Marianne finally did photograph a couple of her new bulletin boards, and these pictures, along with her discipline plan and several bibliographies supplied by the textbook companies, made up her Influences section. Her reflective statement emphasized how difficult and unnecessary this section had been.

For Marianne, though she may not like it, this very thin section of her portfolio served as a concrete and unavoidable testament to the lack of effort she had put into structuring her classroom environment. While painful, it was necessary and useful. Marianne's own comments and difficulties in preparing this section helped her portfolio partner point out to Marianne how little of her own fingerprints were on her classroom. Marianne's supervisor would need to give her concrete suggestions for improving her classroom. If these improvements are made, then Marianne's students will benefit. If not, the portfolio reveals the sparse learning environment she has created for her students.

SUMMARY

Sample Information Included	Sample Items Included
• Classroom environment	• Photos of bulletin boards • Floor plan • Learning centers
• Materials used	• Annotated bibiographies • Computer software lists • Card files • Teacher-made materials
• Discipline methods	• Management philosophy • Discipline plan
• Grouping arrangements	• Classroom schedules • Photos of cooperative groups

REFERENCE

Bloom, B. S. (1964). *Stability and change in human characteristics.* New York: John Wiley and Sons.

CHAPTER 5

Portfolio Development: The Instruction Section

OVERVIEW

THE heart of instruction is the act of teaching, and teaching is the focus of the Instruction section of the portfolio. The first two sections of the portfolio describe the teacher's personal background and the context of teaching. However, the teacher in action is the essence of teaching, and it is this vitality that is the most difficult to portray and assess using our current methods of evaluation.

The Instruction section of the portfolio emphasizes the planning and implementation of lessons. It takes into account the tremendous diversity in students, curricula, and teaching styles. It includes the planning activities teachers use, the materials they use to teach the lesson, and evidence of teaching as it takes place in an authentic setting. The Instruction section is the part of the portfolio that best portrays the teacher in a three-dimensional, human way rather than as a series of marks on a checklist.

ORGANIZING PRINCIPLES

- Three teachers develop their Instruction sections.
- Successful instruction in the classroom takes many forms.
- The Instruction section may include items that describe planning activities, materials used in classroom presentations, and videotapes of actual lessons.

- Reflection on these entries should include a critical self-analysis of what the teacher hopes to accomplish and how well this is being done.

PLANNING THE INSTRUCTION SECTION

Gary Donovan's Plan

When Gary began his teaching career last semester, he was intent upon making his class relevant for his students. For his college prep classes in American literature, that meant teaching his students the skills in critical reading and formal written composition that they would need to be successful in their college studies, as well as introducing them to literary classics. In tech prep the goal was twofold. In addition to reading and composition skills, he wanted to teach the communication skills his students would need to succeed in a two-year, career-related program at Twin Cities Community College, where nearly all the tech prep graduates enrolled after high school. The balancing act was proving formidable.

He decided to organize his American literature course around thematic units, instead of the usual chronological outline that the adopted textbook encouraged. The first unit on genealogy was a hit, and the group presentations on ethnic groups quickly unified the group. He followed with a unit on satire where he worked in the whole range of literary types—some short stories by Mencken, a novel by Twain, some lyrics from contemporary music, as well as some current journalistic writing. The students didn't respond as enthusiastically as he had hoped; however, they seemed to enjoy the assignment where they all wrote a Dave Barry–like spoof on a typical cafeteria lunch. Likewise, the unit on Transcendentalism went well; but he quickly saw that he had dug too deeply into philosophy for sixteen year olds. The reading journals of the students revealed that he had been shooting way over their heads. In fact, his mentor teacher pointed out that he needed to confine classroom discussions more to the students' daily experiences.

Although his tech prep course was turning out to be a logistical nightmare, it was as much fun as the American literature classes. He was delighted that several local businesses were eager to help out. He had students keep portfolios of their work, and periodically several business managers would come in and evaluate the students' work. When he did the bar-coding unit, each of the groups was evaluated by a pair of managers, whom he had his students call their "project consultants." It seemed as though the students took the criticism from the business managers a lot more seriously than they did his routine grading. The training video that one group had done for the bar-coding unit was fantastic! The group had decided to take a comedic approach to the script and staging, and the finished product was as entertaining as it was informative. Even though the video production was fairly amateurish, the training tape showed the kind of creativity, organization of ideas, and attention to detail that he was trying to teach. The students were thrilled when the store manager told them that he would like to have their resumés on file for when he had some openings.

Gary's proudest accomplishment with his tech prep class was the progress most of the students were making with computer technology. Within half a semester they were using most of the features of the word-processing software he had installed on the computer network. They were also using some simple graphics programs to enhance their written assignments. Gary was particularly proud that they were learning computer skills as quickly and as proficiently as his college prep students were.

Still, Gary was perplexed about how to orchestrate his class. With all the cooperative learning and individual activities he had going on, he was frustrated by the number of students who just did what they were told, when they were told. Even though Dr. McIntyre had given him a pleasingly satisfactory evaluation when she made her first observation last December, the videotapes he made of his teaching every few weeks were blunt about this aspect of his classes that he still considered a weakness.

Carmen Garcia's Plan

A typical day in Carmen's classroom starts with a not-so-typical activity—group singing. Carmen has found that songs are an ideal way for her bilingual students to improve their oral and written language skills. She writes the lyrics to each song on chart paper and points out the written words as the students sing. Some songs are in Spanish, and some are in English. She adds new songs periodically and revisits old favorites often. The singing leads naturally into the language arts block that takes up a large part of Carmen's morning.

Carmen plans her teaching in thematic units, and her language arts activities revolve around the themes. The literature she uses and the activities she plans emphasize the themes she selects. In one of her units the unifying theme is the study of Native Americans. The whole class is reading *Island of the Blue Dolphins* together, and they all respond to the book in some way. Response activities are assigned to the students according to their reading abilities and their English language skills. Those students who are ready for more advanced work convert the book into a readers'-theater format. Students who are still transitioning from Spanish to English meet in a small group to work on specific reading skills. Eventually, Carmen plans for all of the students to work toward a dramatization of the book.

After the language arts block, Carmen has specific times set aside in her schedule for mathematics, science, and social studies. She also has specific subject matter in each of these areas that she plans for the students to learn. However, a visitor to the classroom who was unaware of Carmen's schedule would have a difficult time identifying which subject area was being addressed. This is because Carmen's curriculum is so finely integrated. Her principal, Bill Prince, watched Carmen this morning during the unit on Native Americans as she masterfully wove in facts from the social studies lesson about geography and history into her language arts teaching. On other occasions he has seen her incorporate the reading comprehension skill of identifying important details into a science lesson. Carmen's plans reflect that much of this integration is intentional; however, the plans do not begin to demonstrate the level of skill she displays in using the teachable moment.

One other aspect of Carmen's teaching makes it difficult to assess her skill, too. This is the fact that it is not easy to "catch" Carmen teaching, at least not in the traditional sense. True, she is always active. She moves from group to group redirecting, offering insight, pointing out something that has been missed. It is rare, though, to find her standing in the front of the class presenting. Even during whole class activities, a student is as likely as Carmen to take the lead. Carmen's plans show that she knows where she wants the class to go, and her students generally accomplish these goals. However, the route from Carmen's objectives to her students' successful completion is a meandering path that is difficult to describe or characterize.

Marianne Miller's Plan

One thing Marianne is sure about is what first graders need to know. They need to know how to read. Marianne believes that she is paid to turn nonreaders into readers, and this is precisely what she intends to do. She is fairly successful in this endeavor, too.

Marianne decided long ago that reading meant phonics. She believes that if you break reading into tiny enough pieces, even a six-year-old child can do it. Marianne bases her instruction in language arts on this belief. Her plans exhibit how she designs her language arts lessons to teach the letter–sound relationships in words and spends most of the morning teaching and testing these phonics skills. Students meet in three reading groups, according to reading level, and read aloud in order for Marianne to decide if they are learning the sounds and words they need to read. She asks children to sound out words they do not know, and she always plays her sight word game to allow students to practice the words they do know.

While Marianne is meeting with a reading group, she makes sure that she has ample seatwork ready for the other students. This seatwork reinforces the skills in reading that she is teaching. Luckily, the textbook companies provide many worksheets to go along with the books. Marianne likes to use worksheets. They are easy to reproduce, easy to grade, and were designed by "experts." They also demonstrate that her children are learning the skills they need.

Marianne focuses a great deal of her instruction on reading, because it is such a vital area for first graders. However, Marianne does plan lessons in spelling, English, arithmetic, science, social studies, and current events. Each of these content areas (except current events) has a textbook that Marianne carefully follows. The textbooks provide reading material, questions, activities, and unit tests. By using these texts, Marianne is confident her students are being exposed to a sequential, orderly study of each discipline.

Marianne's teaching looks very different from Carmen's, but there is one thing they have in common. Bill Prince finds it as difficult to "catch" Marianne teaching as he does Carmen. Even when he arranges his schedule to arrive at the beginning of one of Marianne's lessons, Bill is likely to see very little actual teaching. Marianne's lessons seem to consist of five-minute introductions to the next set of worksheets. Once she has read the directions aloud to the students, she generally takes her seat at her desk to grade the last set of worksheets while the students work independently. Students occasionally come to her desk to ask a question, but that is the extent of their interaction. Bill finds he has very little of substance to write down about Marianne's lesson.

INSTRUCTION: THE CORE OF THE PORTFOLIO

The Instruction section of the portfolio is the centerpiece of the entire document. Other sections may examine ways to support or modify instruction, but this part of the portfolio provides the actual evidence of teaching quality. As with the other sections of the portfolio, no two teachers' Instruction segments will look alike.

The diversity that makes it difficult to describe and judge good teaching is never more evident than in the actual instruction that takes place in the classroom. Not only do content, grade level, and student needs influence how lessons are presented, but teachers' varying styles and skills also come into play. The same lesson, taught in much the same way by two teachers, could exemplify an extremely high-quality, thoughtful level of teaching for one, while the other merely acts as a technician covering rote material. There is no "right" way to teach, and this will be demonstrated clearly in the Instruction section of the portfolio.

The inclusion of a section devoted to actual instruction is nearly universal in portfolio design. Numerous authors (Berry et al. 1991; Biddle and Lasley, 1991; Vavrus and Collins, 1991) who have advocated various ways of constructing a portfolio have all included some segment that provides concrete evidence of teaching in progress. Some portfolio designs are very prescriptive in the types of evidence that can be used as examples of teaching, while others (Richert, 1990; Wolf, 1991) leave the choice of specific examples up to the teacher. However, it seems to be generally accepted that a teaching portfolio without evidence of actual teaching is incomplete. The quandary becomes how to present concrete evidence of a very fluid activity.

One way to begin documenting actual teaching is to include the written materials that accompany good teaching. Planning and preparation are absolutely essential to high-quality instruction, and these written plans are a natural inclusion in the portfolio. Examples of planning could include brainstorming worksheets, lesson plans, and unit or thematic maps. Depending on the content area and grade level these planning documents will take on different forms. However, the absence of clear appropriate planning will certainly signal inferior teaching.

In addition to documents used to plan, teachers also often include documents used to teach the lesson. Overheads and handouts that support the lesson provide a clearer picture of how the lesson was taught. Worksheets, simulations, questioning strategies, and assignments are also appropriate here. A critique of the strengths and weaknesses of a particular lesson may be helpful. And student products that have been graded by the teacher in an especially insightful way also show how well the objectives of the lesson were met.

Written documents can go only so far in documenting good teaching, however. The strongest way to evaluate teaching is to see it happen. To display teaching in progress, many teachers choose to include a videotape of two or three actual lessons. These tapes should be accompanied by a written explanation of what is on the tape, as well as a critique of the lessons.

The reflective statement in the Instruction section must include a critical analysis of what the teacher hopes to accomplish and how well this is being done. The teacher's educational philosophy should be clearly supported by the actual instruction, or ways to improve this alignment should be addressed.

Now let's look at the portfolios of Gary, Carmen, and Marianne to see how they structured their Instruction sections.

THREE TEACHERS PLAN THE INSTRUCTION SECTION

Gary's Instruction Section

Gary had been so busy getting through his first year that he had not really taken the time to examine whether his teaching was indicative of what he believed about education. His portfolio partner, Allison, focused him in this direction when she began to ask pointed questions about why he had taught a particular lesson in one way rather than another. As Gary considered whether his teaching had any theoretical underpinnings, he was pleasantly surprised to find that he was instinctively following his personal educational convictions. He decided there were three aspects of his teaching that he wanted to showcase in his Instruction section. These were meticulous planning, an emphasis on communication skills, and the integration of technology into his classroom.

Gary's planning was nearly killing him, but he was justifiably proud of the superior lessons he was bringing to his students. His teeming mind and exceptionally wide range of knowledge enriched his teaching. He was able to see relationships between various disciplines and across genres which meant he could easily plan his classes around themes rather than a textbook. He decided to include his planning document for the satire unit as well as one daily lesson plan from this unit. He also got permission from one of his students to include a journal entry that demonstrated how well the student had learned the concepts of the unit.

Gary realized upon reflection that he had placed a high priority on communication skills in his classroom. Granted, the types of skills needed by his American literature students were different from the skills needed in his tech prep classes. Still, this was one unifying feature in an otherwise dichotomous schedule. All of his lessons emphasized communication skills—often in very creative ways. Gary decided his portfolio should include examples of student work from both classes that he had graded specifically to help the students clarify their thoughts. He also put in one example of feedback given to one of his tech prep pupils by a business manager—accompanied by a caption that briefly explained the program that had brought the student and businessperson together.

Another unifying feature to Gary's instruction is his emphasis on integrating technology into every class. He seemed to find new ways each day to use technology in his teaching, and he was grateful for the noticeable progress his students were making. He decided to showcase this aspect of his teaching in his portfolio by including his yearly objectives for computer skills and a student product that demonstrated mastery of these skills.

Finally, Gary found it easy to add a short videotape of his teaching. Since he had been videotaping himself throughout the year, he chose a lesson he had taught near the beginning of the year and a very recent lesson that showed his growth in several key areas. Gary's reflective statement commented on the improvement and changes in his teaching.

Carmen's Instruction Section

Carmen had much more trouble describing what made her teaching good than she did performing good teaching. She had been teaching well for so long, and did so many things instinctively, that it was left to Emily, her portfolio partner, to repeatedly point out instances of superior instruction. Together, Emily and she finally decided to focus Carmen's Instruction section on her convictions that teaching should be integrated and student centered.

Carmen knew that many teachers taught each subject separately with separate textbooks, but this method just didn't work for her. For years now she had done her planning around integrated themes. She was careful to include the necessary skills of her grade level in the curricular areas, and she always planned time each day for every student to listen, speak, read, write, and think. Carmen had ample written evidence that she planned for an integrated classroom. She included in her portfolio a brainstorming worksheet (Figure 5.1), a thematic unit plan (Figure 5.2), a lesson plan highlighting her objectives, and a sample of a student product resulting from the unit (Figure 5.3). She reluctantly allowed Emily to videotape the morning singing and an introduction she did for her students as they began their study of a new author in literature. She included these, along with a commentary, even though as she watched the tape, she could think of a dozen ways she wanted to improve.

Carmen's use of learning centers in her classroom was one way in which she integrated her curriculum and kept it student centered. She changed the centers regularly to go along with the themes being studied. Once the rules and expectations for each center were established, the students were self-directed in using the centers. Carmen decided to include her schedule for center use and refer to her Influence section to show how her curriculum was integrated throughout the day and around her room. She also added a couple of photographs of her students working in cooperative groups to accomplish her objectives.

Carmen's reflective statement discussed how she carried out her philosophy of education in her classroom practice. In general, she was very pleased with the way her teaching had evolved. However, she also noted in this reflective statement how difficult it was to always meet the needs of both English- and Spanish-speaking students while remaining

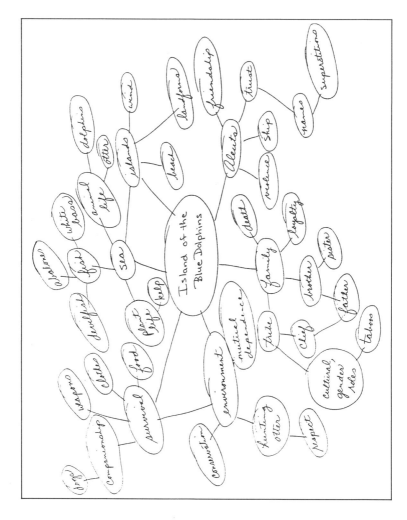

Figure 5.1 *Item from Carmen's Instruction section – brainstorming worksheet.*

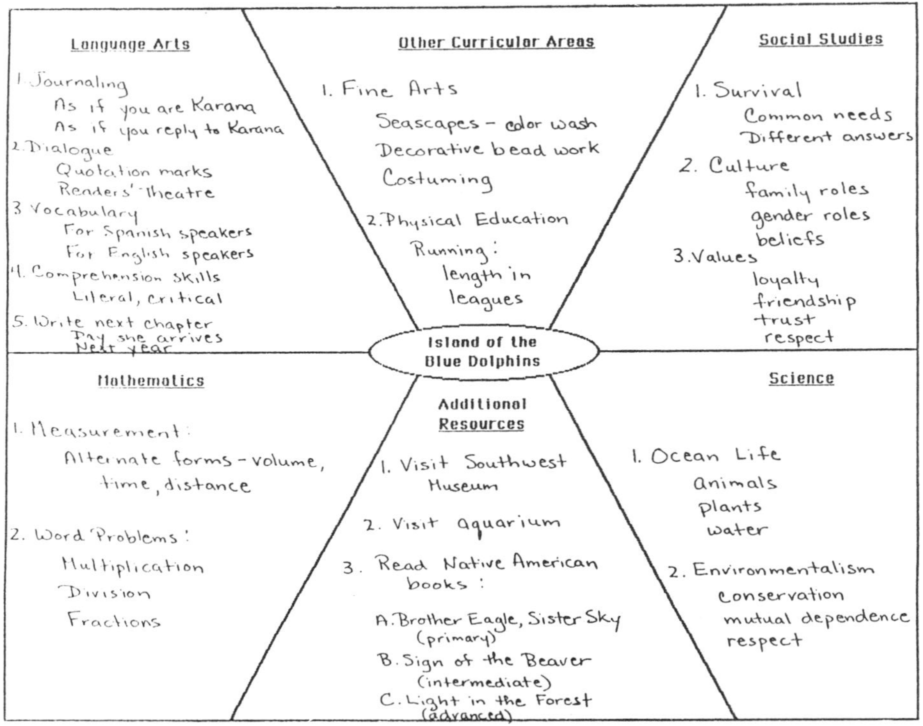

Language Arts

1. Journaling
   As if you are Karana
   As if you reply to Karana
2. Dialogue
   Quotation marks
   Readers' Theatre
3. Vocabulary
   For Spanish speakers
   For English speakers
4. Comprehension skills
   Literal, critical
5. Write next chapter
   Pursue arrives Next year

Mathematics

1. Measurement:
   Alternate forms – volume, time, distance
2. Word Problems:
   Multiplication
   Division
   Fractions

Other Curricular Areas

1. Fine Arts
   Seascapes – color wash
   Decorative bead work
   Costuming
2. Physical Education
   Running:
   length in leagues

Island of the Blue Dolphins

Additional Resources

1. Visit Southwest Museum
2. Visit Aquarium
3. Read Native American books:
   A. Brother Eagle, Sister Sky (primary)
   B. Sign of the Beaver (intermediate)
   C. Light in the Forest (advanced)

Social Studies

1. Survival
   Common needs
   Different answers
2. Culture
   family roles
   gender roles
   beliefs
3. Values
   loyalty
   friendship
   trust
   respect

Science

1. Ocean Life
   Animals
   Plants
   water
2. Environmentalism
   conservation
   mutual dependence
   respect

Figure 5.2 Item from Carmen's Instruction section—thematic unit plan.

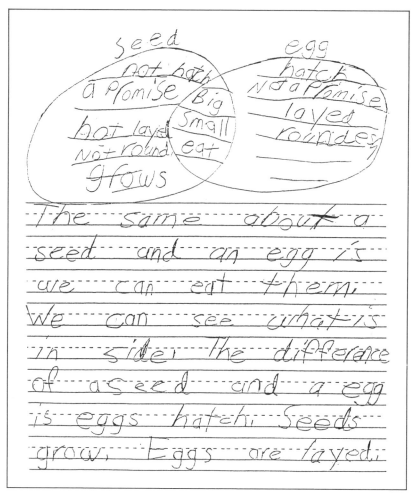

Figure 5.3 Item from Carmen's Instruction section — student product.

committed to her curriculum. This was an area Carmen identified as one she would like to improve.

Marianne's Instruction Section

It is becoming more and more clear that Marianne's portfolio is going to describe a very marginal teacher. Marianne is not ready to recognize this, of course, but others are beginning to see the obvious. John, her portfolio partner, is noticing a pattern beginning to emerge. Marianne has almost nothing to put in her portfolio. Her first section was brief and impersonal; her second section was also slim and depended heavily on published materials. Now, it appeared the Instruction portion was going to be more of the same.

Marianne was having great difficulty producing evidence of thoughtful teaching because she put very little thought into her teaching. She used only the school-issued planbook to do her planning. This planbook was sufficient for her because she followed her texts closely, and her brief plans consisted of textbook page numbers. There wasn't room to write down objectives, modifications, or additional ideas, but Marianne thought all of this planning was unnecessary. She firmly believed that texts were meant to be followed; any material not in the text wasn't really important. She decided to add a page of her planbook to her portfolio because she lacked anything more meaningful.

John worked hard with Marianne to help her identify strengths in her teaching and was gratified to note that Marianne was teaching in a way that matched her philosophy, that is, basic skills should be the core of the curriculum. With so much time and emphasis placed upon phonics, basic sight words, and addition and subtraction facts, Marianne's students were meeting success in these areas. In some instances this was resulting in rapid, word-by-word reading, but at least they were able to identify the words. And even though they might not understand the underlying concepts, most of her students were beginning to develop rudimentary arithmetic skills. Marianne decided to include a few of her favorite worksheets and several unit tests to confirm that she was teaching the curriculum. She also added last year's standardized test-score summaries to show that her students were learning.

Unfortunately for Marianne, this strength was the only one she could identify. John tried to question her about her own creative ideas, alternative ways to plan, or lessons she had designed, but Marianne did not see the need for these things. And she firmly refused to have her teaching videotaped. She felt she had to draw the line somewhere on this portfolio nonsense.

SUMMARY

Sample Information Included	Sample Items Included
• Planning of lessons	• Lesson plans • Brainstorming worksheets • Schedules
• Implementation of plans	• Audio or videotapes of lessons • Handouts and worksheets • Overheads • Assignments • Student products • Photos of students working
• Integration of curriculum	• Thematic teaching units • Curriculum maps • Learning centers

REFERENCES

Berry, D. M., Kisch, J. A., Ryan, C. W., and Uphoff, J. K. (1991). *The process and product of portfolio construction*. Paper presented at the annual meeting of the American Educational Research Association, Chicago.

Biddle, J. R. and Lasley, T. J. (1991). *Portfolios and the process of teacher education*. Paper presented at the annual meeting of the American Educational Research Association, Chicago.

Richert, A. E. (1990). Teaching teachers to reflect: A consideration of program structure. *Journal of Curriculum Studies, 22,* 509–527.

Vavrus, L. and Collins, A. (1991). Portfolio documentation and assessment center exercises: A marriage made for teacher assessment. *Teacher Education Quarterly, 18* (3), 13–29.

Wolf, K. (1991). The schoolteacher's portfolio: Issues in design, implementation and evaluation. *Phi Delta Kappan, 73* (2), 129–136.

CHAPTER 6

Portfolio Development:
The Individualization Section

OVERVIEW

THE evidence of good teaching ultimately is in the success of the student. The most completely planned and expertly delivered lesson will be of no value if it fails to cause the student to learn. While no teacher can expect always to meet perfectly the individual needs of every student in the class, the proof of good teaching occurs when it can be shown, over time, that the majority of students are reaching their full potentials. The Individualization section of the teaching portfolio directly addresses student achievement as a measure of teaching effectiveness.

There are many ways to exhibit attention to individual student learning, and most fall into three basic areas: classroom organization, student assessments, and adaptations of lessons. The Individualization section of the portfolio is perhaps the most diverse section because it invites teachers to explain how they accommodate diversity. All of the assessments and adaptations will be specific to grade level and context. Classroom organization will be in response to teacher style and student needs. Teachers will be judged and will judge themselves on how well they facilitate the learning of the specific content they teach to the specific students who sit in their classrooms.

ORGANIZING PRINCIPLES

- Three teachers develop their Individualization sections.

- The ultimate proof of good teaching is student learning.
- The Individualization section includes items that describe classroom organization to meet individual needs, student assessments, and adaptations of lessons to accommodate needs.
- Reflection in the Individualization section should focus on how well the teacher's goals for individual students are being met.

PLANNING THE INDIVIDUALIZATION SECTION

Marianne Miller's Individualization Plan

Marianne has been teaching first grade for a long time, and she has seen many children come and go. A few have been somewhat memorable but most seem very, very similar to her. Almost as soon as she gets a new class in the fall, she can pick out the students who will give her discipline problems, the ones who won't be able to keep up academically, and the ones she can depend upon as helpers. Every year it's the same thing, and the predictability of children is a comfort to her. Marianne falls back on this experience every time the subject of individualization comes up. Sometimes she hears it more than others, but her response has always been the same, "Teaching is like bowling—you aim for the middle and hope for the best." Any time someone questions this philosophy, Marianne cites years of teaching experience to back up her claim.

Marianne sees children as more similar than different, and she arranges her room and instruction to go along with this point of view. Everyone follows the same textbooks at roughly the same pace. Everyone gets the same assignments that are evaluated with a consistent standard. Everyone takes the same tests. Everyone abides by the same rules. Of course, she does notice that, unfortunately, all the children are not at the same reading level, so she keeps three reading groups going in her room. These groups go through the same materials and are taught in the same way, but she increases or decreases the pace of instruction depending on the children's abilities.

The consistent way in which Marianne runs her classroom has paid off for her in many ways that are important to her. It has cut down on her workload quite a bit. She prepares one lesson per subject area, one assignment, and one evaluation. Even in reading she manages to prepare only once, even though she uses each lesson three times after she gets all of the groups moving along.

Marianne treats every child equally. If a student gets a poor grade on the end-of-the-unit test, then Marianne is assured that the child deserves the poor grade. There are no special treatments in her class, and it is easy to explain to parents how she determines grades.

Marianne is happy that her consistent rules have resulted in an orderly classroom. She has seen other classrooms that accommodate individual needs for movement or space, and she thinks this leads to chaos.

Marianne's principal thinks that Marianne may be using the concepts of consistency and fairness to rationalize some fairly mediocre teaching methods. He has several pieces of evidence that concern him. First, he is concerned about the standardized test scores from Marianne's class. He has noticed a disturbing trend. While the average children achieve the average scores he expects, the slower children and the children who are above average do not show much progress at all. Consequently, he believes that the needs of these children are not being met adequately.

The second thing that disturbs Mr. Prince is the parent complaints he regularly receives about Marianne's classroom. He is well aware that every teacher will have the occasional parent complaint, but Marianne's parent woes are excessive and seem to have a great deal of merit. One parent reported that her daughter was ridiculed when she didn't know the answer to a question. The child said that Marianne told her that she was supposed to be the class genius and should know the answer. Another angry parent complained that Marianne told her child not to ask questions because "smart children don't need to ask questions." Even if all of the complaints Mr. Prince hears aren't true, he still has to admit that Marianne's room is much more subdued than any of the other first grades. Somehow all the children have turned into quiet, faceless clones, and Mr. Prince doesn't think six-year-old children normally behave this way.

Gary Donovan's Individualization Plan

Not long after Gary began teaching he noticed that some teachers taught the same lesson the same way to every class, and he promised himself that he would not slide into that routine. He knew that his students had different abilities, different personal interests, different learning styles, and different goals after high school. The challenge was to juggle all his tasks so that he could really teach the way he knew that he should.

For example, in his American literature course he required each student to keep a reading journal. He told his classes that the only standard he intended to use when he graded the journals was whether they showed that the writers were seriously reflecting on whatever they were reading outside of class. The students were required to turn in their journals every three weeks, and they were supposed to have at least ten new entries. Gary always planned to use his time on the weekend that journals were due to write short responses in the margin. This was his way of having a private conversation with the students about their wide ranging interests in reading. Also, he found that many students who were reluctant to make candid comments in class discussions used the journals to probe ideas much more deeply than they would in front of their peers. "Journal weekend" really cut into his personal time, but the writing and thinking that the students did showed him that it was worth it.

Gary also used writing portfolios in his American literature classes so that students and their parents could see the progress they were making during the year. The English department at Emerson High School used the "process approach" to writing, so every essay went through several revisions before its final evaluation. Often he used peer critics for early stages of the process, and he was pleased with the improvements that he could see in the quality of his students' compositions.

In his tech prep classes he also used student portfolios for evaluation. The contents of the tech prep students' portfolios varied widely, depending on their special projects. Students were encouraged to select roles in their group projects that played to their strengths. In the project where a group was preparing a personnel manual, two students drafted the policy statements, and another worked on the word processing and page layout.

His computer system that enabled students to look into his electronic grade book anytime turned out to be a real hit. He had the system set up so that students could see only their own grades, and they could print out the summaries anytime they wanted. He thought this took the mystery out of how grades are decided and made students more accountable. Also, he found it very handy for communicating little problems to parents before they became big problems.

Despite all of Gary's enthusiasm, his extraordinary work ethic, and his technological know how, he still was frustrated with a few students who just did not have the aptitude to be successful in the activities that he had planned. Like all the high schools in his state, Emerson had just started a policy of inclusion, and Gary found that he was unprepared to help some of the students who were enrolled in his tech prep classes.

Carmen Garcia's Individualization Plan

Carmen shares many philosophical views with both Gary and Marianne. She agrees with Gary's work ethic and tries to impress that upon her students. She agrees with Marianne's ideas that consistency and fairness are important in the classroom. Carmen has her own style of teaching that embraces these ideas without leaving her exhausted or rigid. Her classroom style is based heavily on the individual needs of her students, a fact that she does not fully realize.

One of the first things that Mr. Prince notes about Carmen's classroom is the warmth. There is an easy respect between the teacher and students. She does not ridicule them; they do not taunt her. It is obvious that the room functions as a family, with genuine high regard for each member.

Carmen knows her students well. She knows them well academically through a variety of assessment measures. She uses not only the standardized tests available to her through her district but also many authentic means of evaluation. Her students keep journals, they write books, and present projects. She uses informal reading assessments to discover the students' reading abilities. She keeps a card file of their interests and achievements in literacy. All of these measures, plus her professional observations, give her a good idea of what each of her students knows and needs to know.

Carmen also knows her students well personally. The questions that she asks each one as they come through the door show that Carmen knows, remembers, and cares about the personal concerns that the students are experiencing. She also allows her students to know her a little on a personal level. When they brought in baby pictures of themselves so did she. When her son was sick, she told her students; they asked about him every day. This personal respect seems to be the basis for the trust with which Carmen and her students approach their academic tasks.

Carmen does not always realize how much she knows about each child or how well she has earned the trust of the class. However, she is very deliberate in two areas that relate to individualization. The first area, brought on by necessity, is the language development of her students. All of her students are literate in their first language by now. However, in terms of English literacy her students range from the student whose first language is English and is capable of doing above grade-level work to the student who is transitioning from a first language to English to the student who just immigrated and has no knowledge of English at all. Obviously all of these students will not benefit from the same instruction. Carmen, therefore, uses many techniques to help the non-English speakers acquire English at the same time as she teaches much of her grade-level content in both Spanish and English.

The other tool Carmen uses regularly to individualize her classroom is the learning center. Carmen has centers that change regularly, such as the weather center that went along with the weather unit. She also has centers that are available all year, such as the writing center or the listening center with bilingual tapes. By having a variety of centers with a variety of assignments and activities, Carmen has found it much easier to meet the multitude of individual needs in her class.

THE INDIVIDUALIZATION SECTION OF THE PORTFOLIO

According to Bird (1990) any teaching portfolio should address four areas: responsibility, subject matter, individual students, and class organization. While all of these areas will be a part of each section of the portfolio, a portfolio using the five I's devotes one section specifically to meeting the needs of individual students. In this section of the teaching portfolio, the teacher is less concerned with the overall planning and delivery of a basic lesson and more concerned with the lesson's impact upon individual students. The teacher is asking: How well did that lesson work? Which students did not understand what I was trying to teach? How can I better reach my students to improve my efficiency? In asking these questions it is obvious that teachers will not only need to evaluate their delivery skills but will also need to evaluate student achievement.

There are three basic ways to demonstrate individualization within the classroom. One important aspect of any classroom is the way in which it is organized to encourage individual success. Many organizational systems lend themselves to dealing with students as individuals. Whatever organizational strategies a teacher uses to individualize should be outlined and explained in the Individualization section. Some examples of the ways in which teachers organize for individual needs include the use of cross-age tutoring, learning centers, resource rooms, or other special assistance for students. Other examples of individualization are differentiated curricula, assignments, or assessment strategies. Teachers are often unaware of how important their classroom organization is in terms of individual student achievement. As they move through the Individualization section of the portfolio, they often realize how they have fostered or inhibited individual student growth through their classroom organization and become more deliberate in the way they organize for instruction.

A second way in which individual student learning can be evidenced is through assessment techniques. All teachers evaluate their students for progress, and so the very first item teachers often think of putting into this section is testing. This is a good start, but testing by itself is not adequate. The Stanford Teacher Assessment Project (Wolf, 1991) lists evaluating student learning as an important component of any teaching portfolio, and the Individualization section of the portfolio is a natural place to include student evaluation. However, a list of test scores or a sheaf of tests will be of limited value without an explanation of what the teacher learned from these results and how this information was used. Evidence of student learning includes standardized test results, teacher-made test results, anecdotal records about students, authentic assessment products such as student projects, and assignments that the teacher has graded. Shulman (1992) emphasizes the importance of including student work—both good and bad—in any teaching portfolio. The product of teaching is student learning and can best be proven through student achievement.

The final area that should be addressed in the Individualization section of the portfolio is the adaptations the teacher makes in response to student needs. Having evidence that students have different skills and needs is of no value unless teachers use this knowledge to improve instruction in some way. Shulman's (1992) advice to include poor student work in a teaching portfolio is a good example of how a teacher uses the knowledge that the student has not learned what was taught. Exactly what action was taken by the teacher to help the student to learn the content after it became apparent that the lesson had failed? How was the lesson retaught? What feedback was given to the student? A graded and corrected homework assignment would be a good example of how a teacher used student evaluation to assure student achievement. Examples of written work that have gone through several revisions show student learning as it is taking place. A cycle that displays an assess-reteach-reassess method of teaching shows how the teacher is using knowledge of student needs to deliver effective lessons.

Adaptation of lessons can be done in a variety of ways and is not always done only in response to a student blunder. Most teachers differentiate their curricula in some way to take into account the different learning styles, abilities, and interests of their students. They might accommodate differences in as simple a way as varying the rate of instruction. Some students will receive the instruction in a slower or quicker way than others. Teachers can vary the assignments by asking several levels of questions or vary the way in which they assess knowledge by giving an oral test to a student with limited reading skills. In each of these examples, the teacher has taken the time to determine the needs of the student and has found ways to help the student succeed in the classroom. The teaching portfolio should provide evidence of these and other ways in which a teacher successfully reaches his or her students and should also provide evidence that the teacher is always striving to improve student achievement through more effective teaching.

Marianne, Gary, and Carmen each approached the Individualization section of the portfolio in a highly individual way. This seemed completely fitting to their mentors who already saw them as very unique teachers.

THREE TEACHERS PLAN THE INDIVIDUALIZATION SECTION

Marianne's Individualization Section

Marianne found the Individualization section of the portfolio to be the easiest one so far. This was a relief to her because all of the other sections had been so difficult. True, she did not plan a great deal of individual teaching for her classroom, but she did have a great deal of assessment going on. It was relatively easy for her to include many evaluations of her students in this section.

Marianne decided to focus on the three areas of the Individualization section that had been included in the portfolio in-service session at the beginning of the year. These areas of organization, assessment, and adaptation seemed to be a straightforward way to address the limited individualization she deemed necessary in her classroom. As far as organization, Marianne had two ways in which she individualized—both born out of necessity. Since her children were not all at the same reading level, she had been forced to divide the class into three reading groups. She had accomplished this by using the recommendations of the kindergarten teachers and by using the readiness-test scores she had received at the beginning of the year. In her portfolio, Marianne placed a list of students in each reading group with the test score next to each name. Marianne also had helpers from the high school to read with her class. Two high school students from the future teachers club were assigned to every first-grade teacher, and Marianne added the names of her student helpers and the days they were scheduled to work to her Individualization section.

Assessment was an area in which Marianne had plenty of information for her portfolio. She used the standardized tests given throughout the school, end-of-unit tests that came with her textbooks, and lots of workbook pages that she always graded. She chose to include a listing of standardized test scores for her class. She also decided to include a few of the graded workbook pages. This seemed a little silly because the answers were in the book, but it did show that her students were working.

The adaptation part of this portfolio section proved to be a little more difficult for Marianne. She talked it over with her portfolio partner to see if he could help her. John suggested that she include ways in which she had used the test results to inform her teaching, but she could not think of any time when the test results had changed her lesson plans. If a student got a poor grade on an assignment, she recorded a poor grade and communicated this eventually on the report card. Unless the whole class wasn't catching on, as had been the case recently with missing addends in math, she saw no reason to keep going over and over a concept until everyone understood.

John also suggested that Marianne think of ways in which she had communicated individually either with a student or his parents. Parents have a vast knowledge of their child and can help a teacher determine individual needs. Unfortunately, Marianne felt it was better to avoid parent contact as much as possible. She finally decided to include a copy of her planbook that showed that she was teaching the three reading groups at different rates – and decided not worry further about adaptation.

Gary's Individualization Section

Gary had achieved a great deal of individualization in his classroom, and the workload was taking a toll. His entire first unit in American literature had been based upon the cultural heritages of the students in his class. The unit had gone a long way toward motivating the students, but it had been nearly impossible to plan and deliver. Since this unit was an exceptional example of using his students' interests to teach course content, Gary decided to include the bibliography he had assembled in the Individualization section of his portfolio.

In American literature, Gary also realized that he was doing a great deal of individualization through his use of student journals. His comments on the students' thoughts were insightful and led the students to think still more deeply about their reading. These journals also let him know his students better, which was no small task with the numbers of students in his teaching load. Gary decided to include a few examples of journal pages that he thought showed that a student had gained a particularly strong understanding of the reading. He made sure that the pages he chose also had comments from him that demonstrated how he interacted with his students through their writing (Figure 6.1).

As Gary was going through his students' journals in search of likely entries, he began to remember all of the time he took to help his American literature students write, edit, and rewrite their work. He decided to include a particularly gratifying example of student work that had begun at a relatively low level but been polished into a very nice essay. Along with the actual first, second, and final drafts of this essay, Gary included an explanation of the writer's conference he held with the student as he progressed through the revision process.

Gary used his computer to individualize the reporting of grades to students and their parents. He was justifiably proud of this innovation and included an explanation of it in his portfolio. What made him happiest, however, was the feedback he continued to receive about the system. He had gotten a particularly gratifying computer message from a parent who was pleased to be in such close contact with a teacher. With permission, he copied this note and included it in his portfolio as further proof of his success in meeting individual needs.

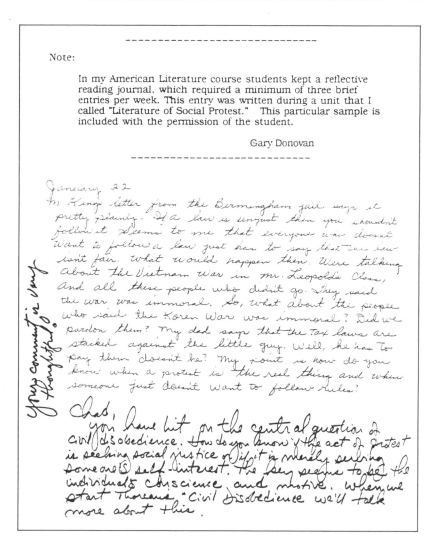

Figure 6.1 Item from Gary's Individualization section—journal entries.

As Gary worked through his Individualization section with Allison, he was not only reminded of the many ways in which he used the knowledge of his individual students to inform his teaching but also of the ways in which this knowledge was not being used effectively. He was painfully aware, for instance, that some students in his tech prep class were floundering terribly. He was also aware that his emphasis on cooperative work was allowing a few of his American literature pupils to slide by with minimal work. Gary decided to make reaching all of his students one of the major goals for his second year of teaching. He hoped that his next teaching portfolio would show progress in the Individualization section.

Carmen's Individualization Section

Until Carmen sat down with her portfolio partner, she was not really aware of the many ways in which she accommodated the individual needs of her students. Emily was the one who pointed out that the very organization of Carmen's classroom demonstrated a commitment to individual needs. Carmen's learning centers were specifically designed to be used by students of varying literacy levels. The centers were organized around the curriculum of the fifth grade, and the activities within the centers addressed different learning styles, abilities, and levels. By making different assignments from the centers to different students, Carmen could be sure that each student was receiving instruction at the correct level in the correct manner. This goal would not have been nearly as easy to achieve if she had tried to teach the same curriculum in a whole-class, lecture method. Carmen decided to include her yearly planning document that showed how her learning centers were arranged to enhance the fifth-grade curriculum. She also decided to list the activities she had designed for one center with notations about how each activity addressed the individual learning of her students.

Carmen had a great deal of student assessment and student work that she could include. Her problem turned out to be one of selection. Carmen's classroom was filled with student projects, student writing, and student work-in-progress, and it was difficult to choose the best exhibits of student growth due to her teaching. Of course she had the standardized tests, but to be perfectly honest, these did not show that her students were experiencing as much growth as she thought they were. The tests failed to measure the exceptional strides her students were making in becoming literate in a second language, because the tests were designed for students whose first language was English. Also, the tests were totally inadequate in telling Carmen if her students were becoming more creative, more self-directed, or more divergent in their thinking. These were important goals to Carmen, and she was always disappointed when the standardized test scores judged her students as "adequate."

Instead of the standardized test scores, Carmen decided to include several examples of the informal and ongoing assessment that she did in her classroom. Carmen kept an index card for each of her students on which she listed their reading levels in both languages, interests, and recent literature work. She also noted the reading conferences she had held with the student. Carmen put one of these cards in her portfolio (Figure 6.2). Carmen also did an informal reading inventory with her students periodically throughout the year. This not only demon-

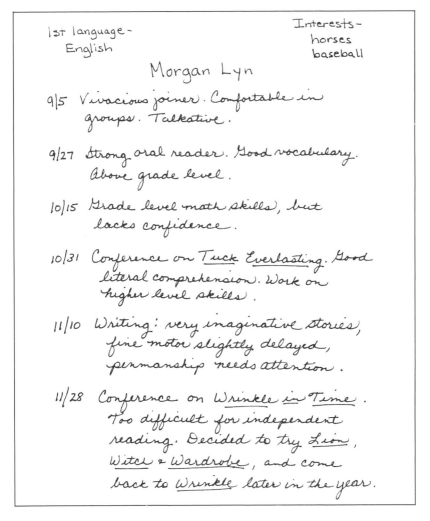

Figure 6.2 Item from Carmen's Individualization section – individual student file card.

strated to her the reading level of each child, but also gave her clues as to what skills the student still needed to improve. She included a page from one of the reading inventories with her analysis of the miscues alongside (Figure 6.3).

Finally, Carmen decided to place some carefully selected student work in her portfolio. She intentionally chose a paper of a student who was working exclusively in Spanish, a paper of a transitioning student,

She fled once more to her rock which seemed to be suspended above the sea. For long hours, as the lullaby of the waves filled her ears, she considered her decision. Did she have the courage to leave everything she had always known just to find her colors? It would certainly be less dangerous to remain the sheltered girl of the village. And perhaps she really was colorless inside, in which case it would be better to never find out such a horrible thing. Once again she wished with all her heart to have fine flashing eyes the color of cocoa, so that she could lead the life of a normal villager.

Hesitation — before unknown words. Word attack skills used to decode.

Omissions — usually not meaning-changing.

Repetitions — only to establish comprehension after a corrected word.

Phonics skills in evidence & used often. Initial consonants used routinely.

Comprehension — excellent even with a multitude of mistakes because most did not change meaning.

This informal reading inventory was administered to the student at the beginning of the school year. Miscues are noted in the text and summarized along the side.

Figure 6.3 *Item from Carmen's Individualization section — sample informal reading inventory.*

and a paper of a student who was fluent in English. Each of these papers was accompanied by Carmen's remarks to the student that clearly demonstrated her awareness of the learning needs of each child. In her reflective statement, Carmen pointed out how her teaching style reflected her teaching philosophy that children should be met where they are and taken from there. She was also careful to explain how inadequate the standardized tests were in measuring the progress of her students in the areas she deemed were most important.

SUMMARY

Sample Information Included	Sample Items Included
• Classroom organization	• Grouping arrangements • Learning centers • Use of special resources
• Student assessment	• Student work samples • Evaluation instruments • Case studies • Feedback from others
• Lesson adaptations	• Differentiated curriculum • Assessment accommodations • Individualized assignments • Feedback to students • Revised student work

REFERENCES

Bird, T. (1990). The schoolteacher's portfolio: An essay on possibilities. In J. Millman and Linda Darling-Hammond (Eds.), *The new handbook of teacher evaluation: Assessing elementary and secondary school teachers.* Second edition. Newbury Park, CA: Sage, 241–256.

Shulman, L. (1992). *Portfolios for teacher educators: A component of reflective teacher education.* Paper presented at the annual meeting of the American Educational Research Association, San Francisco.

Wolf, K. (1991). *Teaching portfolios: Synthesis of research and annotated bibliography.* San Francisco, CA: Far West Lab for Educational Research and Development. (ERIC Document Reproduction Service No. ED 343 890).

CHAPTER 7

Portfolio Development:
The Integration Section

OVERVIEW

THE true value of a teaching portfolio is that it allows teachers to look at teaching in a holistic way. Teachers assess their own work in terms of the content of teaching, the context of a specific classroom, and the needs and styles of all the participants. According to Lee Shulman (1992), one of the chief beauties of the teaching portfolio is that it allows reflection upon teaching beyond a single lesson or snapshot of a teacher at work. The Integration section of the portfolio is the piece that supports and mandates the holistic approach.

In the Integration section a teacher is asked to pull together the seemingly disparate parts of teaching to make a unified picture of a teacher at work. The section includes thoughts about an educational philosophy as a base for defining the type of teacher the teacher hopes to be and items that prove that these ideals are being followed. The Integration section is the vehicle for summarizing and reflecting upon the type of teacher that has been described in the previous four sections of the portfolio. The Integration section also makes the process of teaching improvement a spiral of never-ending growth. In this section, the teacher spells out goals for improvement that will form the basis for later evaluations.

ORGANIZING PRINCIPLES

- Three teachers develop their Integration sections.
- The Integration section provides the unification of the portfolio.

- The Integration section has three main goals: to delineate the teacher's definition of good teaching, to use the evidence in the rest of the portfolio to prove these ideals are being met, and to plan for improvement.
- The Integration section may include items that describe the educational philosophy of the teacher; awards, honors, and evaluations that show expertise; and goals and objectives for continued professional growth.
- Reflection in this section should unify the teacher's vision, hopes, and plans for professional growth.

PLANNING THE INTEGRATION SECTION

Gary Donovan's Integration Plan

By midspring Gary had accumulated a drawer full of materials that he could include in his portfolio. He had unit plans and lesson plans, evaluation guides he had developed for student projects, samples of students' writing with his evaluative comments, and photographs of class activities. He even had edited a videotape so that he could show segments of his teaching in different situations—introducing new subjects in a lecture, leading class discussions, facilitating small groups, and even tutoring individuals. Of course, he had the report from the one formal observation that his principal, Dr. McIntyre, had reviewed with him; two evaluation reports from his department head, Karl Mortensen; and the notes from several class observations that his portfolio mentor, Allison, had given him. He had samples of the forms he had developed for communicating with his students' parents, complimentary letters from the businessmen and businesswomen that he had asked to help evaluate his students' tech prep projects, as well as a note he had received from a parent thanking him for the extra attention he had given one of his students. The portfolio would be easy to shape into final form, and he was confident it would show him to be the kind of teacher he was trying to be.

Ah, what kind of teacher was he trying to be? When Gary met with his mentor to talk about tying everything together, that was the first thing she asked. As well as he knew Allison, he remembered the sheepish sound his voice made and the rambling answer he gave her—an answer that made no more sense to him than it did to her. Allison told him that platitudes and jargon wouldn't work. "Explain to me in as few words as possible what defines you as a teacher—the beliefs you hold about students and teaching and learning. Then, we can see whether all this stuff you have piled up matches your goals."

During the rest of the meeting with Allison, his mind wandered as he began thinking for the first time what he really was trying to accomplish as a teacher. The question seemed to stimulate his thinking for the rest of the week, and finally he sat down and tried to put onto one page his statement of beliefs about teaching and learning. He promised himself that he would avoid the clichés and pseudo-intellectual jargon that had turned him off when he had a similar assignment in his education classes only a year ago.

When he finished, he showed the piece to Allison. She was genuinely impressed with his sincerity. Then, after the compliments, she challenged him one more time. "Come up with a list of your strengths as a teacher, but stick to the evidence you have accumulated for your portfolio," she said. Then she added, "Make another list of any aspect of your teaching that you want to try to concentrate on as an area you should improve."

Again Allison admonished him to stick to facts—the examples and documentation of his work. "Whatever you say about yourself ought to be obvious from the things you'll be putting in your portfolio."

Immediately Gary remembered the comments from Dr. McIntyre's evaluation. "Too many students are on the fringe of attention," she observed. "Only a part of the class was truly engaged." And Karl's advice all year long was to try to keep activities tied together somehow. Of course, he really was proud when the Chamber of Commerce gave him a recognition award and used his tech prep class as an example of how schools and business should work together.

When Gary finished his list, he found that Allison wasn't finished. "You know," Allison mused, "the only excuse we can have for doing this is to take an honest look at ourselves and then come up with a plan for becoming better. Let's come up with a practical method of doing something about the parts of your teaching that you want to improve—goals on one side; ways to accomplish those goals on the other."

Carmen Garcia's Integration Plan

By the time Carmen was ready to begin the final section of her portfolio, she was noticing that the process of designing a portfolio had already begun to influence her teaching. In her classroom, she was asking herself why she taught a particular lesson in a particular way far more often than she had done before she began to keep her portfolio. She was gratified to find that her instinctively designed and presented lessons went along with her personal philosophy of education, but it was a new experience to step outside intuition and really examine the way she taught. However, she did not have a written philosophy of education, and she recognized this as a problem. In the past this had not seemed really necessary because things always went well in the classroom. Now, as she began the Integration section of the portfolio, the lack of a clearly articulated philosophy of teaching seemed to inhibit Carmen's ability to set goals.

Carmen's portfolio partner saw this problem coming before Carmen did. Carmen's room was a wonder to behold, and she clearly had specific notions about how children learn and should be taught, but each time the subject of a unifying vision for Carmen's classroom came up, Carmen dismissed it as unimportant. Emily was very gratified, therefore, when Carmen brought in her slender Integration section and broached the subject of educational philosophy.

No other section of Carmen's portfolio had been slender because Carmen's teaching was so active and diverse. However, the enormity of her teaching style was the very thing that was making it most difficult for Carmen to unify her teaching. How was she to decide what was important about teaching for her when so many things seemed vitally important? How was she to set goals when all of these important things cried out to be done at once? With so many children needing so many different things from her, how could she prioritize their needs? These conflicts caused Carmen a great deal of thought. She desperately wanted to make a difference to each one of her thirty-four students, and she felt that she was doing that to a great extent, but she could not seem to see how all the pieces fit in order to make a complete teacher. Emily had known that Carmen would struggle with the Integration section because she also had struggled there. When a strong, energetic teacher is asked to explain what she does instinctively, the answers are often difficult to put into words.

Emily began by asking Carmen to look at all the other sections of her portfolio and make some observations. For instance, in the Influences section, what did Carmen's classroom environment say about her teaching? Carmen could see that she believed children should be active in their learning, that they should have choices in what and how they learned, and that they should be encouraged to work together whenever possible. These observations, as well as thoughts about the other sections of the portfolio, became the beginning of Carmen's philosophy of education.

Going through her portfolio section by section accomplished something else for Carmen, too. From watching her classroom unfold throughout the year, Carmen began to see clear patterns and specific areas of strengths and weaknesses. This helped her to begin to set goals and prioritize what she could and could not do as one teacher in a class of thirty-four students. Carmen went back into her classroom more focused from her work on the Integration section, and she hadn't even finished it yet.

Marianne Miller's Integration Plan

Marianne's classroom was perhaps the most easily described and the most seemingly organized of our three teachers. Since Marianne's curriculum was based primarily on textbooks, she had no trouble organizing or prioritizing her instruction. The textbook companies did this job for her. Almost all of her instruction was done with the whole class, and therefore her scheduling and planning seemed very straightforward. On the surface, Marianne seemed to be very sturdy in knowing what and how she should teach.

Marianne also had a ready philosophy of education. She had heard it years ago in her foundations of education class and had adopted it as her own. The one-line statement fit nicely into the two-line space in which school district applications asked for your educational philosophy. Her philosophy read, "A teacher should take each child where she finds him and move him along as far as she can." This sounded fine to Marianne, and she had never been questioned about it. She had the happy impression that the Integration section of the portfolio was going to be no problem at all to complete.

This happy impression didn't last long, however; her partner, John, asked her to prove she was following her philosophy by using the other sections of her portfolio. She stuttered through a few marginal pieces of evidence and finally said she would need to think about it. Next, John wanted her to use her philosophy to guide whatever goals she wanted to set for improving her teaching. Her big goal up to now had been to become tenured. Improving her teaching had not been her focus. Again she told John she would need some more time to think.

John was encouraged by the fact that Marianne wanted to think more deeply about her Integration section. He tried to help by asking her to reexamine her educational philosophy to make sure it really said what she believed. He also encouraged her to use the rest of her portfolio to prove she was teaching to her philosophy. Goals would finally become clear, he assured her.

Marianne went away anything but reassured, however. She had thought she was on the verge of finally finishing her portfolio only to find out that this section was going to be as bothersome as all the others. She complained to her husband that this portfolio thing was taking so much thought she couldn't think about teaching.

THE INTEGRATION SECTION OF THE PORTFOLIO

Mary Diez (1994) once referred to the portfolio as a sonnet, a mirror, and a map. She used these three images to explain the uses of a teaching portfolio. According to Dr. Diez,

> The portfolio offers encouragement for reflection in at least three ways. First, it provides both the discipline and the freedom of structure, allowing one to see one's own work. Second, it provides the opportunity to assess one's own strengths and weaknesses through examination of a collection of samples, as well as to get feedback on one's performance from others. Third, the process of self-assessment leads one to setting goals for future development and professional growth.

All three of these functions of the portfolio are fulfilled in the Integration section. This section unifies all of the teacher's knowledge and learning. It is the section in which the teacher reflects most deeply on what it means to be a good teacher and whether he or she is attaining this standard. In fact, all of the other sections of the portfolio could be viewed as merely serving as evidence for the Integration section, for it is in this section that teachers must decide upon their worth in the classroom.

There are three main goals of the Integration section. First, all of the discrete functions and beliefs about teaching that have been evidenced in the first four sections of the portfolio must now, somehow, be pulled together to form a picture of a complete teacher. This is not an easy task, and beginning teachers and veterans alike have difficulty. Good teachers have a functional philosophy of teaching and may even have the philosophy of education paper that they were required to write in college, but many very fine teachers teach every day without ever giving serious thought as to why they teach as they do. Without this unifying vision, though, it is difficult for teachers to make choices, to set goals, and to improve their teaching in any intentional way. This is inhibiting for a good teacher, but may not be seen as very important because good teaching is taking place. However, for the marginal or struggling teacher this unifying philosophy is vitally important. Lacking a strong philosophical base and also lacking intuitive teaching skills, these teachers have very little chance of making more than the most superficial of improvements. The first goal of the Integration section, then, is to compel a teacher to form a unified vision for education.

For most teachers this unified vision means a philosophy of education. Although the philosophy of education might reasonably be included in other sections of the portfolio, most teachers choose to include it in the Integration section. This individual education philosophy not only links together all that the teacher believes about education but also provides a core of principles against which past and future teaching can be measured. This philosophy then serves as the base for all future decisions in teaching and is the necessary first step for goal setting.

The second function of the Integration section is to compare what the teacher has done in the past with the self-professed philosophy to see how well practice is matching intent. The first four sections of the portfolio should provide ample evidence of the type of teaching going on in the classroom. Now the teacher's task is to ask whether the way he or she is teaching actually supports this educational philosophy. Besides the evidence provided in the rest of the portfolio, there are other ways to prove that teachers are living up to their ideals. Many teachers put evaluations from administrators or department heads in this section. Some teachers ask a peer or mentor to observe their teaching and make comments to include in the portfolio. Notes from parents or students that are specific enough to provide insight into teaching could be included here. Awards, honors, or honorary societies that support the teacher's philosophy would go in this section. Finally, but probably most importantly, the teacher's self-assessment of performance in relation to ideals is a necessary inclusion in the Integration section.

The third function of the Integration section is goal setting. The main reason why teaching portfolios are used is the improvement of instruction. The weak teacher is improved or removed, the beginning teacher is helped to become a professional, and the strong, veteran teacher is encouraged to grow. In all cases the goal is to improve instruction. Teachers who look carefully at their skills, think deeply about their strengths and weaknesses, and decide upon their most important goals are going to be much more motivated to change and improve than the teachers who merely respond to the wishes of others outside the classroom. A mentor, or portfolio partner, can be invaluable in this process, though in the end it is the teacher's self-assessment that forms the basis for goal setting.

Most teachers use the documentation provided in the other sections of the portfolio as a natural foundation for setting goals for self-improvement and for selecting strategies to reach these goals. These goals should be both short and long term and should be closely aligned with the teacher's educational philosophy and identified weaknesses. This set of goals is a natural place for discussions between the teacher and the principal on how to improve the classroom before the next evaluation. It is also a measure that can be used later to see if improvement has in fact taken place and whether the goals have been met.

Reflection is a vital part of becoming a good teacher. Indeed, the National Board for Professional Teaching Standards, which is responsible for developing standards for national certification, is considering establishing the importance of reflective practice as one of its standards for the early childhood/generalist credential. The reflective statement in the Integration section should be the strongest, most introspective piece in the entire portfolio. All that the teacher is, hopes to be, and plans to accomplish will come together in the Integration section. This reflective statement, along with the specific goals set by the teacher, make the portfolio into a continuous spiral of self-reflection and self-directed improvement. Teachers should realize that the portfolio is never truly finished. It is always a work in progress, just as becoming a teacher is a work in progress. The conclusions reached in the Integration section serve to catapult the teacher to a higher level of expertise.

The three teachers we have followed throughout the book are now to the point of completing their Integration sections and coming to the end of the first try at their portfolios. They are radically different teachers, as has been shown all along the way in their portfolio development, and these differences will be most evident in their Integration sections.

THREE TEACHERS PLAN THE INTEGRATION SECTION

Gary's Integration Section

Gary spent a great deal of time, at Allison's insistence, preparing his educational philosophy. He had already developed one educational philosophy when he began his portfolio last October. It seemed like an eternity ago, and Gary was pleased to see that his thoughts this spring are more solid and mature than the notes he had written in the fall. He decided to replace the philosophy he had included in his Introduction section with this new philosophy. He still did not agree, however, that the philosophy should come at the end of the portfolio, so he decided to leave it at the beginning. He thought referring to it in the Integration section would help draw the whole portfolio together. Allison explained once again that this was fine as long as he had given thought to why he was doing things a little differently than others might.

Since his philosophy of education was not going to be included in the Integration section, Gary had to decide what he would include. He referred back to his portfolio in-service guide and found that the section often contained evaluations, honors, and goals.

He included the formal evaluations from his principal and department chair. Both observers had made lots of positive comments and noted some areas for improvement. Gary used these evaluations to set his goals for improvement. Gary also had a number of informal observations that he could include in his evaluations. Allison had observed his teaching numerous times at his request, and each time she had written a short critique of what she had seen. Gary had found these collegial visits even more helpful than his formal observations because there was less pressure and more emphasis on just improving his teaching. He had used Allison's comments to make immediate changes in his classroom almost every time she had visited. Gary also had one more type of informal evaluation: the unsolicited notes from his students and their parents. Several times during the year Gary had received complimentary notes, and he decided to include one such note that was very specific about how he had helped a student.

In the area of awards, Gary was pleased to be able to cite the commendation his tech prep project had received from the Chamber of Commerce. He also thought this might be a good place to put a couple of the letters he had received from businesspeople who had taken part in the tech prep class.

Finally, the whole portfolio came down to one important task—the settling of goals. Gary gathered up his beliefs about what education should be, his evaluations from other people, the evidence presented in the rest of his portfolio, and his self-evaluation of his videotape. Then he hibernated for a day in his study. It almost seemed like too much information to assimilate. How was he to decide upon goals for next year and beyond when all of his teaching was so scattered? Nevertheless, as he examined and reexamined the documents he had spread all over his desk, he began to find common themes.

One of the themes he noticed immediately was that his philosophy espoused a passion and excitement about learning that was evident in his teaching. Learning should be interesting and engaging to students. He believed this strongly, yet he also saw how this passion had been one of his major problems. He was personally interested in so many things that he had failed to focus his classroom. He had tried so hard to use student interests in his teaching that much of what he did was fragmented. He had tried to do too much too soon, and sometimes his teaching was disconnected, not to mention exhausting. One of Gary's goals then was to plan fewer activities but plan them better and in a more integrated way.

Another general theme Gary noticed, especially when he viewed his videotape, was that many of his students were not fully engaged in his lessons. As he was teaching a lesson, it was hard for him to notice how many students were not paying attention, but as he watched his tape he was discouraged at the number of disengaged students. He thought deeply about why this was true and began to notice that it especially happened when too much was going on in the room at one time. Perhaps focusing his activities more tightly would also help his students to take more of an active role in his classroom. This became another goal.

Slowly, working his way through his portfolio and through the afternoon, Gary identified the parts of teaching that were of most importance to him, the areas of strength in his teaching upon which he could build, and the goals for improvement that would make the most difference in his classroom. At the end of the day, he had finished his list of goals, as well as his reflective statement for the Integration section. He was ready for his meeting with Dr. McIntyre.

Carmen's Integration Section

Carmen had a difficult time with her Integration section. This took her by surprise because she had always been proud of the way she had been able to integrate her curriculum. However, it turned out that integrating her teaching was a formidable task. The idea of looking at the rest of her portfolio for guidance didn't help much because she had so many entries in so many different areas. Emily's advice to begin with a philosophy of education proved to be more helpful. It took Carmen quite a lot of time, but she was finally able to put on paper her major beliefs about teaching. She found this task to be extremely satisfying—after it was over. She included her philosophy of education at the beginning of her Integration section.

The second part of her Integration section included all of her evaluations. Most of these were the formal observations made each year by her principal, but because she had been teaching for so long, she had a great number of evaluations. She decided to include only observations from the last five years and then in her reflective statement to point to ways in which she had used these evaluations to improve her teaching. She also had numerous notes of thanks and praise from parents and students. These seemed too much like bragging to her though, so she included only one note from a student that had deeply touched her (Figure 7.1).

The awards section made Carmen even more uncomfortable. She had been honored several times in her career by her school and by the district. These awards had made her happy and humble at the same time, and she did not want to include them in her portfolio. Emily encouraged her to at least refer to these awards in her reflective statement, but Carmen was adamant and did not mention her awards in her Integration section.

Finally, Carmen also faced the idea of self-evaluating her teaching well enough to establish goals for improvement. She thought this would be easy. She always had about a hundred projects she wanted to complete, and there was always some workshop on a new teaching idea that she wanted to attend. Setting her goals didn't turn out to be easy, however. Yes, she had many, many interests, but narrowing them down proved to be a problem. As Carmen looked through her portfolio she began to see trends that could eventually become important goals for improvement.

One trend that Carmen could not ignore was that her classroom was so busy, active, and noisy that some children were not thriving. Those children who needed quiet or solitude in which to work were not being well served by her bustling classroom environment. Yet this active way

Figure 7.1 Carmen's note from a student.

of teaching was important to Carmen and not something she wanted to change. She decided to make meeting the needs of her less social students while not giving up an important tenet of her teaching philosophy one of her goals for next year.

Another goal that Emily was finally able to get Carmen to accept was the idea of beginning to help other teachers. Carmen had so much skill and so many good ideas that other teachers naturally came to her for advice. Carmen was happy to help on an informal basis but had resisted all attempts to take a position of formal leadership. Her refusal was partly due to Carmen's self-effacing attitude and partly due to shyness. Carmen finally began to realize that she had a great deal to offer other teachers. She decided to make serving as a mentor teacher to a beginning teacher one of her goals for next year and also to run one small workshop on techniques for teaching bilingual students. Carmen finished her Integration section with a strong reflective statement and was ready to schedule her yearly supervisory conference with Bill Prince.

Marianne Miller's Integration Section

Marianne breathed a sigh of relief that she at least had her philosophy of education out of the way. Everyone else she talked to seemed to be taking a great deal of time with this exercise; they were having real difficulty in getting a philosophy onto paper. Marianne thought they were all working too hard on a simple task, but she decided to keep her thoughts to herself.

The problem came for Marianne when John told her that she needed to be able to provide evidence that she was teaching according to her philosophy and that this evidence should already be in her portfolio. As she looked through her portfolio, Marianne wasn't sure what she was proving about her teaching, but she was pretty sure there wasn't much evidence that she was following any sort of philosophy. Instead her portfolio seemed to be proving that Marianne's philosophy of taking a child where you find him and moving him as far along as possible was not informing her teaching at all. Her portfolio showed a teacher who did not look carefully at the needs of individual students, did not plan curriculum around student interests or needs, and did not move many children as far as their potentials would allow. This meant that Marianne either needed to change her teaching style or her philosophy of education. She could tell that doing either of these things was going to be a great deal of trouble.

The fact that Marianne began to notice the dichotomy between what she professed made a good teacher and the teacher she actually was, was a step in the right direction. It would only be of value, however, if it caused Marianne to change her teaching. Unfortunately, Marianne was not ready to do the work necessary to make herself a better teacher. After she realized that she was not living up to even her own idea of what made a good teacher, she pushed this knowledge aside and finished her Integration section in the same perfunctory way that she had completed the other sections of her portfolio.

She included her philosophy of education, her evaluations from Bill

Prince, as well as all of her evaluations from her former principal, a letter of commendation that her former school had given her when she moved, and a short list of personal goals. The goals included such items as gaining tenure, learning to use the new adopted math textbook, and being more creative. She wasn't sure about the being creative part, but Mr. Prince had put it on every one of her evaluations so she thought it would be a good idea to include it as a goal. Marianne could tell that her portfolio partner wasn't exactly satisfied with her Integration section, but she believed that he had been highly critical all along. At least the job was done; she was ready to hand the whole thing in to her principal and be done with it.

SUMMARY

Sample Information Included	Sample Items Included
• Statement of personal beliefs	• Philosophy of education
• Evidence of growth	• Formal evaluations
	• Peer evaluations
	• Self-evaluations
	• Notes from students and parents
	• Awards and honors
• Plans for continued growth	• Goals for improvement
	• Plan of action

REFERENCES

Diez, M. E. (1994). *The portfolio: Sonnet, mirror and map.* Paper presented at the Linking Liberal Arts and Teacher Education: Encouraging Reflection through Portfolios Conference, San Diego.

Shulman, L. (1992). *Portfolios for teacher educators: A component of reflective teacher education.* Paper presented at the annual meeting of the American Educational Research Association, San Francisco.

CHAPTER 8

Using Portfolios for Evaluation

OVERVIEW

THE essential value of a teaching portfolio is its benefit to the teacher who prepares one. If a portfolio does not cause reflection by the teacher and if it does not foster collegiality among teachers, then the process has not been properly utilized. Teaching portfolios should not become a dreaded instrument of evaluation. Instead, they should be a tool for professional development.

Nevertheless, portfolios do have a place in the evaluation process. Indeed, the disenchantment that teachers have with typical evaluation methods has spawned much of the interest in teaching portfolios.

When portfolios are used for the evaluation of teachers, we must follow some basic principles. This chapter discusses the use of portfolios in the teacher evaluation process. Basic concepts of teacher evaluation are reviewed in the context of evaluating teaching through the medium of the teaching portfolio.

ORGANIZING PRINCIPLES

- Three teachers complete their portfolios.
- Evaluate the teacher, not the portfolio.
- Establish the purpose of the evaluation.
- Develop the rubrics for the evaluation.
- Train the evaluators.
- Validate the evaluation process.

COMPLETING THE PORTFOLIOS

Gary, Carmen, and Marianne were at different points in their careers when they began their portfolios.

Gary was a first year teacher, and he had little in the way of teaching experience. He was going to show his portfolio to his principal at the end of the year in conjunction with the mentoring process for first-year teachers.

Carmen was a veteran with an abundance of successful experience behind her (and ahead of her as well). She was using the portfolio as a way to invite others to help guide her professional development.

Marianne also was beginning the year with plenty of previous experience. However, her purpose for beginning the portfolio was different from either Gary or Carmen. She was preparing the portfolio in conjunction with her evaluation for tenure.

Each teacher began the portfolio project with a very different purpose in mind. The several different ways that their mentors helped them prepare for evaluation illustrate how varied evaluation by portfolio can become.

Gary Donovan Reflects on the First Year

Gary felt more at ease on his way to Allison's room than he had when Dr. McIntyre reviewed her evaluation of his work. He didn't conduct a good class the day she observed him, and he regretted not having the chance to show her what he could really do. Even his two sessions with Karl, his department head, intimidated him a little. Karl was a nice guy, but he seemed to spend more time talking about departmental curriculum matters and orders for supplies than talking about Gary's teaching. Gary had been working with Allison on his portfolio all year now, and they had already discussed what was working and what was not. When he got there, Allison had already poured a cup of coffee for him and had his portfolio on her desk.

"Have a pop-tart, Gary."

"Pop-tarts in the afternoon? What's this?"

"Yeah, well I brought them this morning to have for breakfast during second period, but second period sort of flew by. Do you want one or not?"

Gary's lunch break went the same way as Allison's second period, and he accepted the offer. As he was unwrapping his late lunch, Allison opened his portfolio.

"You know, you are a good teacher Gary. I mean, a really good teacher. I picked up a lot of ideas just looking through your portfolio. When I read over your professional development plan at the end, I could tell that you mean to follow through. You're going to be a great teacher."

Gary beamed inside when she emphasized the words *good* and *great*. It had been a tough year, and by March he was worn out. That whole month he had doubts about whether he wanted to stay in teaching. Having another teacher understand and appreciate what he had been trying to do was what had kept him going. The pop-tart was delicious.

"Well, I'll tell you, Allison, I didn't much want to do this at first. I mean, I was surviving hour by hour when I started. But I'm glad I did. So, what did you think about the portfolio?"

"Ah! You're like your kids after all, aren't you? You want to know your grade. Well, your grade is . . . I think it's ready to show your Beginning Teacher Review Committee. It shows you at your best, and it shows you as wanting to get better."

Gary was pleased that Allison was complimenting him. By now they pulled no punches with one another, and he knew she was being candid.

"How about if we go over it piece by piece. Tell me what you like and what you don't like."

For the next hour or so, Gary relived his whole first year: his very best unit, "The Age of Anxiety," that he spent most of Thanksgiving vacation planning; the radio show his tech prep class had planned and broadcast at a local station; the individual conversations he had with students about their reading journals; the terror that ripped at his poise when Dr. McIntyre came for her observation. He remembered Dickens's immortal opener: "They were the best of times. They were the worst of times."

As they talked, Gary found it easy to agree with Allison's comments. Even when he didn't agree, he saw that her different viewpoint was helpful; it helped clear up his own thinking about what he was trying to show, and whether it was worth showing. Her criticism of his video was right on target; he had edited it in a hurry, and he knew it wasn't ready to show anyone. Also, he could see how someone who hadn't been in his class would not understand the photo page that showed the skit his literature class put on—the modern version of *The Scarlet Letter*. (What a riot! He smiled as he wondered how he escaped parent complaints over that one. Next year he'll definitely give better directions.)

He explained to Allison why he chose to organize his portfolio a little differently than the way they were trained. He had two separate Instruction sections—one for his college prep American literature class and one for his tech prep class—and she asked why he moved his philosophy of education statement from the last section to the first. Her only real criticism was that he should include some student essays that he had graded, complete with his remarks to students on them. By the time their meeting ended, Gary realized that he had talked with her about what he was trying to accomplish as a teacher, and together they had evaluated whether the materials he had included in his portfolio revealed his values and his skill in transferring those values to his classroom.

As they were finishing, Allison asked Gary if he would be willing to help a new teacher start a teaching portfolio next year.

Gary thought about all the hours Allison had spent with him and started to say that he just didn't have the time. Then, he thought about how helpful those meetings had been.

"Sure!"

Carmen Garcia Selects the Best of the Best

As the end of the school year approached and the due date for the portfolios loomed, Carmen was relieved to see that her own portfolio was beginning to find its final shape. She had numerous documents in all five sections of her portfolio, and she had spent a great deal of time on each reflective statement. These statements had caused her to think deeply about her own views of teaching in a way she hadn't done for years. As she reread each of the statements, she was pleased with her ability to identify and express her deepest thoughts. Carmen was eager to share this nearly finished portfolio with her portfolio partner, Emily. They made plans to meet in Carmen's room, because Carmen's portfolio now consisted of a three-ring binder, a photo album, and a large box and wasn't that easy to transport.

Carmen and Emily had a wonderful time warmly remembering the year that was almost over. Carmen had eight pictures of the Halloween parade, pictures of the bulletin boards she had used all year, writing samples from nearly half the class, and examples of twelve of the many units she had developed. This was the first time Emily had seen the portfolio in its entirety, and it proved to be a little daunting. It also seemed to be too much like a memory book, which was not the purpose of the portfolio. Emily knew she would need to help Carmen see this flaw. She decided to start with a question.

"This portfolio certainly reflects a teacher who is energetic, creative, and loves to teach," began Emily. "What do you like the best about your portfolio?"

Carmen paused a long moment to consider. "You know, I enjoy looking at the pictures of the kids and their work," she said, "but the most valuable part for me, professionally, is the reflective statements. I understand myself much better now than I did when I began this."

"I think you're right," replied Emily, "your writing shows real introspection. The reflective statement in your introduction, the one in which you show how your early experiences influenced your teaching, is just a masterpiece. You should be serving as a mentor, because you really understand teaching. Now, what would you consider a drawback of your portfolio?"

"It's too hard to carry!" laughed Carmen without any thought.

"Yes, it is a little overwhelming," agreed Emily. "Maybe you should take some things out."

"But, what could I take out?" protested Carmen. "Every one of these pictures or units is a happy memory."

"Yes, they all make me smile," replied Emily, "but what if we used a different measure besides memory to decide what stays? I think you should ask yourself what each item demonstrates about your teaching that has not yet been shown in the portfolio. Do the pictures of the Halloween parade tell anything about your teaching? Let's take them out," Emily said as she started to remove the pictures.

"Hold on," said Carmen, "all my kids came dressed as their favorite book character for that parade, and we tied it into our literature lessons."

"In that case," said Emily, "let's leave one of the pictures in and clearly label it so that anyone could easily see what this picture says about your teaching."

And so Carmen and Emily worked together to begin the difficult task of editing Carmen's portfolio. They moved slowly through each section, deleting the redundant items and labeling all the remaining ones. When they finished, Carmen's portfolio was a graphic, yet manageable, record of her strength as a teacher.

Marianne Miller Gets It Done

The longer this silly portfolio thing carried on the more vexing Marianne found it. All year long she had to collect ridiculous items, go to special meetings, and meet repeatedly with her portfolio partner, John. He was supposed to be helping her complete this time-wasting project, but as far as she could see he had been just another in a long line of aggravations. Each time she met with John, he pushed her to examine her teaching, and her own thoughts about teaching, more deeply. Well, today was her last meeting with him, and it was a good thing. She planned to just get everything into a folder and get rid of it. She had been teaching for over a decade, and she didn't have time for all this thinking!

John was worried about Marianne. He had tried all year to help her grow as a teacher, and she rebuffed him at every turn. This might not have been so worrisome if she had been doing a better job of teaching first grade, but as it stood, many of her skills were inadequate. She firmly refused to acknowledge this and was growing more defensive about the portfolio each time he saw her. Today he had decided to be as straightforward as possible, since tact did not seem to be producing the desired results. He could see when she walked into his room that it wasn't going to be a friendly, collegial session.

Marianne began, "Let's see if we can't finish this up today because I'm tired of thinking about it. I've wasted enough time on it already."

"I've noticed," replied John, "that you have your portfolio beautifully organized. You seem to have a real skill for orderliness in your classroom, and it shows in your portfolio. Yet you have consistently referred to your portfolio as a waste of time. What is it, specifically, that you are finding so difficult?"

Marianne answered without a moment's hesitation, "There is nothing to put into it. Sure I can put in my resumé, my evaluations from the principal, and my teacher certificate, but everyone else has more. All the suggestions you have given on what to put in don't seem to work for me. Why would I put in a diagram of my regular room arrangement?

Everyone knows what a room full of desks looks like. And lesson plans, what good is it to copy my planbook? I only list the pages I'm covering. The reflective statements are useless, too," continued Marianne. "I've been teaching first grade for a very long time, and I have it down pat. There is nothing to reflect about."

John decided to try one more time. "Maybe it wasn't such a waste of time for you to discover how little of yourself you have put into your teaching," he ventured. "If everything in your teaching reflects only the creativity of someone else, where is your own creativity? If the last time you really thought about what it means to teach was years ago in college, perhaps it is time to think about it again. Maybe it isn't a waste of time to discover these things, and this portfolio could serve as the beginning for real growth in your teaching."

Marianne paused for a moment, and John thought there was a chance he had made an impression. Then Marianne said, "If you could just tell me if you think this three-ring-binder format works, I could get this turned in and we could both forget about it. I need this to get tenure, John. Let's just get it done."

EVALUATING TEACHING THROUGH A PORTFOLIO

Teachers are not satisfied with the current methods of evaluating their teaching. A few observations by a principal do not tell the whole story. Nor does it cause much self-reflection on the part of the teachers. Portfolios are useful for evaluating teaching because they allow a teacher to explain the background, that is, to provide the context. In addition, they create opportunities for teachers to exchange their ideas and present their work in a setting that is supportive and encouraging. Evidence from schools indicates that experienced teachers prefer teaching portfolios to conventional forms of teacher assessment (Tierney, 1992).

However, at some point portfolios are judged by someone other than the teacher. Maybe the teacher is being evaluated for tenure. Or perhaps the teacher is being considered for an award. The reasons vary, but often the consequences are substantial. If portfolios are to prove helpful as an alternative form of teacher evaluation, then the evaluators need to keep several principles foremost in mind.

Evaluate the Teacher, Not the Portfolio

The most zealous proponents of teaching portfolios will admit that it is possible for a teacher to prepare a dazzling teaching portfolio and still be an incompetent teacher. The exhibits may not be representative of the actual teaching that goes on all year, or they may not even be the teacher's own work. In short, it is possible for a teaching portfolio to look better than the teacher. When portfolios are used in the evaluation process, it is essential to evaluate the teacher, not the portfolio.

Several questions will help an evaluator focus on the teacher as revealed through the portfolio rather than judging the craftsmanship of the portfolio itself.

(1) Is the work in the portfolio representative?
   The portfolio should show the teacher at work through the whole year and with the kinds of pupils the teacher actually teaches.
(2) Is the work the teacher's own?
   The portfolio should show that the teacher can plan, implement, and evaluate instruction. If the unit and all the supporting materials, as well as the tests, are from a textbook's resource manual, there is no evidence of the teacher's own creativity and resourcefulness. The instructional materials that are exhibited should be original with the teacher.
(3) Are evaluations from supervisors included?
   The portfolio should be viewed as giving context to external evaluation of teaching. It is not intended to be a substitute for external evaluation. Evaluations from a principal or department head should be included. In addition, the evaluations should come from more than one evaluator. Indeed, they may come from very nontraditional sources, such as letters from former pupils or parents. Summaries of observations by peers should also be included.
(4) Has the portfolio been produced professionally?
   Just as employment consultants are available to prepare resumés, professional assistance is becoming available for portfolio production. While the presentations are slick, they miss the point. The essence of the process is the care the teacher takes in collecting, reflecting, discussing, and organizing.

Evaluations that incorporate portfolios into the evaluation process need to consciously resist the tendency to judge the quality of teaching by the quality of the portfolio. The portfolio must be viewed as a medium that exhibits quality in teaching. It should never be the object of the evaluation.

Establish the Purpose of the Evaluation

Any evaluation of teaching that utilizes the portfolio process must first consider the purpose of the evaluation. When the reason for the evaluation changes, the kind of portfolio a teacher prepares should change.

Most kinds of teacher evaluation that would utilize a portfolio fall into one of five categories:

(1) Evaluation for new employment

(2) Performance evaluation by supervisors

(3) Professional certification

(4) Self-evaluation for professional growth

(5) Consideration for professional awards

When a teacher is seeking employment, the portfolio becomes a very valuable tool for communicating professional skills and personal attributes that potentially distinguish the teacher from the rest of the applicants. The teacher, of course, is trying to showcase talent and make as strong and favorable an impact as possible. On the other side, the administrator or teacher screening committee is trying to gain a deeper insight into the qualities of the teacher that might not be readily evident in a typical interview. As a job applicant, the teacher needs to anticipate the professional qualities and skills that the prospective school desires. Similarly, the school needs to identify those qualities and skills so that they can be pinpointed in the teacher's portfolio. For the teacher, the portfolio is a business proposal: If you hire me, this is what you can expect to get. For the school, it is like a prospectus: If I hire this teacher, this is what I can expect to get. As a result, the evaluation of the portfolio by the administrator or selection committee is a matter of matching up what the portfolio shows and what the school needs.

Performance evaluation calls for a different kind of portfolio and for a different approach to evaluation. When a teacher's professional performance is being considered, specific rubrics, or rules, need to be developed and followed. In this case, the balance between uniformity and flexibility becomes delicate. The portfolio needs to include evidence of essential teaching skills. In addition, the variety of teaching situations and diversity of individual strengths must be accommodated. Typically, a portfolio that is going to be used as the summation of a teacher's professional performance will have many more "required" documents than one that is going to be used for self-evaluation.

More and more agencies and states are beginning to use portfolios as the means to evaluate teachers for professional certification. Whether the evaluation is for the initial teaching credential or for a higher level of professional certification (e.g., certification by the National Board of Professional Teaching Standards), the instructions for the teacher need to be explicit. Both the teacher and the evaluators need to understand the rubrics used for evaluation. As with any evaluation, the validity and reliability of the particular method need to be established.

Portfolios are best utilized as a tool for professional development, in which case they become the teacher's professional self-portrait. When the purpose of the portfolio is to self-assess strengths and weaknesses, the portfolio takes on a whole different character, and the nature of the evaluation changes. The professional development portfolio is the medium by which the teacher, with the assistance of a mentor, describes the kind of teacher he or she wants to be and then takes an honest look at what kind of teacher he or she really is. When used for professional development, the portfolio's evaluation needs to target the kinds of information that will help the teacher plan a personal agenda for professional development. Moreover, when teaching portfolios are used on a schoolwide basis for professional development, they should allow the teacher maximum flexibility.

Teaching awards are yet another use of portfolios, and they constitute another dimension for evaluation. When a group of teachers is competing for an award and portfolios are to be the means by which the selection will be made, then rubrics are again essential. The teachers who prepare portfolios must know ahead of time what values will be applied in the evaluation, and they must know what aspects of teaching are to be emphasized. Of course, the evaluators must know the same. Otherwise, the evaluation of the teacher, as evidenced by the portfolio, deteriorates into a portfolio contest.

Develop the Rubrics for the Evaluation

When portfolios are used for certification or performance evaluation, it is especially important to develop rubrics, or rules, that the evaluators are obliged to follow.

A *rubric* is simply a standard. Just as objective tests have keys, subjective exercises have rubrics so that the evaluation is both valid for the purpose intended and is reliable. An excellent example of the application of rubrics to the evaluation of teaching portfolios can be seen in the process used by the National Board for Professional Teaching Standards (NBPTS, 1994). Teachers receive instructions on what the National Board expects to see in a portfolio and how it should be organized. In addition, evaluators are given guidelines that spell out criteria by which the teacher, as revealed through the portfolio, is to be judged.

Of course, the criteria for National Board certification have been developed expressly for the evaluation of the experienced teacher who seeks a distinguished level of professional recognition. Any other purpose would require another set of specially designed rubrics. A school that uses the portfolio process as part of a professional review prior to tenure would need to develop a unique set of rubrics. Similarly, a state department of education that intends to use portfolios as the basis to evaluate applicants seeking an alternative teaching credential would need to develop rubrics for that purpose. Just as the type and extent of the exhibits would vary, so would the rubrics used by the evaluators. The validity of the evaluation of portfolios depends upon the validity of the rubrics that evaluators apply.

For illustrative purposes only, a set of sample rubrics is provided in Appendix D.

Train the Evaluators

The validity of the evaluation of teaching portfolios depends upon rubrics, and the reliability depends upon the training the evaluators receive.

The evaluation of teaching portfolios is subjective. No apology is needed because it is the subjective nature of the process that allows the teacher to express unique personal and professional qualities during the evaluation. However, teachers and administrators need to recognize that not all evaluators are likely to see the same meaning in a piece of evidence. Subjectivity becomes a prime concern when professional careers are affected by decisions based upon evaluations using teaching portfolios.

If a teaching portfolio is to be used in conjunction with evaluation for career-ladder programs, initial professional licensing, or professional certification, then the training of the evaluators is crucial to ensure the reliability of the evaluation process. While each training program has to vary according to the actual purpose of the evaluation and the specific rubrics that have been developed, several elements should always be present.

- The evaluators should have significant professional experience in the same context as the professional performance being described (e.g., grade level, subject area, school community characteristics) prior to the training program.
- The evaluators should have a common understanding of how the rubrics will be applied as a result of the training program.
- The training should include simulation exercises with actual portfolios.

When evaluators have been trained to apply evaluation rubrics properly, the evaluators' ratings can be very reliable.

Validate the Evaluation Rubrics

Teachers know that it is important to establish the validity of any classroom assessment that they use. If we are going to evaluate students, we make certain that what we have them do in the evaluation exercise signifies the real performance. In other words, we make sure that the "test" represents what we really want students to be able to do. Teaching portfolios are no different. The rubrics used in the evaluation must be validated according to what teachers actually do. Otherwise, the portfolio might not reveal what we intend it to reveal.

When teachers and administrators work cooperatively to develop the rubrics to evaluate portfolios, they must withhold final approval until they are confident that validity has been established. While validation is a tedious, time-consuming process, shortcutting this essential step will jeopardize the success of a program to implement teaching portfolios on a schoolwide basis. Credibility of the process is essential if teachers are expected to accept the change. Moreover, the defensibility of personnel decisions will require it.

SUMMARY

The teaching portfolio is truly an evaluation tool. However, the uses for which the evaluation is intended will vary widely. School districts, state boards of education, and even national agencies use the teaching portfolio to judge the quality of teaching in individual context. An applicant for a teaching position may use a portfolio to present qualifications that a resume and interview do not reveal. A state board of education may use one to verify a level of professional competence for persons seeking alternative teacher licensing. Annual performance evaluations, professional reviews for career-ladder programs, national certifications, and professional development are among the many reasons that teachers create portfolios.

Knowing the purpose of the teaching portfolio—hence, the purpose of the evaluation—is the first step. The actual exhibits that a teacher includes (or, is expected to include) and how the exhibits are judged will hinge on the purpose.

When portfolios are used to evaluate teaching, care must be taken to make certain that it is the skill and art of teaching being evaluated and not the skill and art of portfolio preparation. Rubrics, or rules, must be developed and validated for the evaluation process to achieve credibility with the teachers. Valid rubrics take on even greater importance when teaching portfolios are used in conjunction with personnel decisions.

When portfolios are used to judge a teacher, the evaluators must be trained in the specific portfolio process being utilized. Evaluators themselves need to have mastered the skills they are are evaluating, and they need to be fluent in the many ways that these skills can be expressed. The training process should include simulations and utilize actual portfolios.

REFERENCES

National Board for Professional Teaching Standards. (1994). *Illustrative summaries: Early adolescence/generalist assessment exercises.* Washington, DC: Author.

Tierney, D. S. (1992). *Teaching portfolios: 1992 update on research and practice.* Berkeley, CA: Far West Laboratory for Educational Research and Development and Improvement.

CHAPTER 9

Implementation of Teaching Portfolios as Professional Development Tools

OVERVIEW

SUCCESSFUL implementation of teaching portfolios is more likely to be accomplished if they are introduced as an alternative to some other form of professional development. Also, training of the mentors — the teachers who guide others as they prepare their portfolios — is essential. Portfolios are not a fill-out-the-form type of exercise, and teachers need expert guidance.

Rubrics need to be developed at the level closest to the teachers who will be using them. The more bureaucratic or legalistic that guidelines become, the less likely they will be meaningful to teachers. Of course, the rubrics themselves will depend on the purpose of portfolios in the professional development process.

Finally, teaching portfolios should be viewed as a program for professional development. As with any program, evaluation of how well the program is working should guide future policy decisions.

ORGANIZING PRINCIPLES

- Teaching portfolios should be an alternative, not a mandate.
- Don't hurry — let the idea catch on.
- Train the teaching portfolio mentors.
- Rubrics should be developed at the building level.

- Evaluate the program.
- Portfolios are a useful communication tool in supervision.

PLANNING FOR IMPLEMENTATION

Two concepts—empowerment and evaluation—need to be kept firmly in mind during the implementation of teaching portfolios as a tool for staff development.

Portfolios should empower teachers to evaluate themselves, and they should empower teachers to act on their self-evaluations. All the decisions that administrators need to make in the process of implementing teaching portfolios in a school community should be tested against these principles.

Make Portfolios an Alternative Rather than a Mandate

Teachers are skeptical of mandates from state departments of education or administrative offices, especially when it comes to professional development. Their skepticism comes from too much experience with typical methods of staff development. Examples are numerous, and they often are the source of cynicism rather than renewal.

Typical programs usually include schoolwide or districtwide assemblies with rousing, motivational speakers who leave town as soon as the applause ends; required attendance at workshops teachers had little or no say in selecting; or sales pitches for quick-fix solutions by vendors who have commercial interests. No one should wonder why teachers would balk at a mandate that might read, "All teachers will develop and maintain teaching portfolios." They would balk even if the promulgation added ". . . for their own good."

Teaching portfolios should be allowed rather than required. In his recent review of literature on the use of teaching portfolios, Tierney (1992) noted the importance of making portfolios an alternative.

The options vary, of course. They should be allowed in lieu of other professional development activities that the school district might require. Or, if they are to be used in conjunction with teacher evaluation for career-ladder programs, then they should be available as a form of voluntary professional development that will be taken into consideration when the promotion decision is made. But mandating the use of teaching portfolios is certain to ensure that they will not be taken seriously or ever lead to the professional growth of teachers.

Although a teaching portfolio should be optional, the incentive for initiating and developing one needs to be great enough that teachers will want to learn about them and try them. Several strategies are recommended.

Strategies for Implementation

First, implementation should be targeted at the building level. One of the by-products of teaching portfolios is professional dialogue, and the smaller the community of teachers who plan and complete a portfolio project, the more meaningful the dialogue will be.

Next, the principal should recruit about six to eight teachers who will agree to participate in a pilot project for at least one school year. In the pilot project the teachers will be trained in portfolio development, they will pair off, and they will help each other work on their portfolios. In this pilot phase, a modest honorarium should be awarded to the teachers who complete the process. Of course, grapevine gossip will inform the other teachers about the portfolio project, and they will be watching the dynamics between the paired teachers. Since the "portfolio pilots" will be models, it is very important that they be accepted by their peers. Having portfolio pilots who represent different stages of a teaching career is also helpful.

The teachers from the pilot phase will become mentors to other teachers who wish to build teaching portfolios. As the others begin, they will then have the assistance of a portfolio mentor who has been trained and who has already prepared an actual teaching portfolio. Teachers who volunteer in the second phase will have observed the portfolio pilots, and they will be seeking the same benefits – the opportunity to engage in self-evaluation, support from a peer mentor, and self-directed professional development.

The second group of teachers who volunteer to use the portfolio in their professional development should also receive incentives. As with the pilot phase, modest honoraria can go a long way. At this time, the process needs to be proposed as an option to either the standard professional development program or the regular method of reviewing teachers in conjunction with career-ladder decisions.

Train the Mentors First

Unless the first wave of teaching portfolios is high quality and the dynamics that produced the portfolios is conducive to sustaining professional growth, the benefits of using teaching portfolios in a school will be lost. The group of teachers who were selected should meet before the school year begins for some hands-on training. Although many different formats can work, one in particular is recommended.

A project leader, preferably a classroom teacher known to the participating teachers, should conduct the training. Although all the concepts can be covered in one day, the training needs to be more than a show-and-tell session. It needs to be hands on and should take about three days. Teachers actually need to create a framework for their portfolios and begin discussing possible exhibits. They need at least two days for group activities that produce actual outlines and sample rubrics.

Moreover, the project leader cannot just pack up and leave after the initial training. Several follow-up sessions need to occur during the year. One in the fall should allow the teachers to share with one another how their portfolios are going to be organized. Also, by the fall sessions rough drafts of the reflective statements should be completed. By February a preliminary list of exhibits for each of the sections should be completed, and many of the exhibits themselves can even be collected. In April or early May, the portfolio should be nearing completion. In this session teachers can show what they have done so far and invite feedback from the group.

Of course, the formal follow-up sessions do not replace the ongoing conversations that occur between the teacher pairs. Rather, the follow-up sessions are an opportunity for the group to gain the guidance and feedback they will need from the project leader.

By the end of the school year, the portfolio pilots should have their first teaching portfolios ready to use. In addition, they will be ready to begin serving as portfolio mentors to the second round of volunteers.

Develop Rubrics for Evaluation

Rubrics, or rules, for the evaluation of teaching by portfolios need to be developed at the level closest to the teachers who will use them. The more remote from teachers the formulation of rubrics becomes, the less likely teaching portfolios will be taken seriously by the teachers who will be preparing them.

Once the principal has provided for the training of the pilot teachers and once they each begin their own portfolios, those teachers, the principal, and the project leader should formulate the rubrics they will use. Only in that fashion will the teachers have the unequivocal confidence that their teaching will be evaluated through their portfolios in a way that will be meaningful.

Empowering teachers to develop teaching portfolio rubrics at the building level is vital to deriving the real benefits of self-evaluation and self-initiated professional development. In this regard, the process is as important as the product. When a project leader facilitates a discussion on the meaning of good teaching and the verifiable evidence of good teaching, the teachers begin to absorb the values they articulate in the process as part of their own professional ethos.

The teaching profession should resist the temptation to adopt a bureaucratic frame of mind for developing rubrics for teaching portfolios. No matter how well-intentioned or how well-fashioned, rubrics from a state department of education or a large school district office that promote uniformity in teaching portfolios miss the point. The teaching portfolio must be the individual teacher's personal expression of his or her individual teaching qualities.

Of course, the rubrics need to reflect the purpose. Rubrics for teaching portfolios used in conjunction with personnel decisions, such as evaluation following the beginning year or a recommendation for tenure, will be different than those used as part of teacher assessment for professional development. However, both sets of rubrics need to be the product of the teachers' collaboration. And the teachers' collaboration should be assisted by a facilitator who is experienced in portfolio assessment of teaching.

As part of the implementation process, rubrics for evaluating teaching with portfolios should be developed by the pilot teachers and the project leader early in the pilot year.

Evaluate the Program

Teaching portfolios should cause teachers to reflect on their own teaching, foster a collegial approach to teacher assessment, and stimulate self-directed professional growth. How well they accomplish these goals should be the basis for evaluating a teaching portfolio program.

Program evaluation for the use of teaching portfolios in a school is an indispensable part of the implementation process. Program decisions must be informed by our accurate observation and interpretation of experience. Evaluative judgments of a formative nature discourage the continuation of practices that impede progress toward the program's goals, and evaluative judgments of a summative nature support valuable progress and eliminate ineffectual programs. When implementing teaching portfolios as a tool for professional development, a program evaluation cycle of no less than three years should be planned.

A Time Line for Implementation

Implementing teaching portfolios as a tool for professional development must be viewed as a gradual process. It begins with a few teachers who use portfolios effectively and then model portfolio assessment of teaching for other teachers. Consequently, a time line of at least three years should be allowed for complete implementation. Figure 9.1 includes a recommended time line for the events that should be included in the implementation plan.

PORTFOLIOS AND THE PROCESS OF SUPERVISION

The word *supervision* is derived from two Latin words meaning "to see more." In factories of yesteryear, supervisors actually stood on platforms above their workers so that they could, literally, see more. However, modern industrial and organizational psychologists have redefined supervision to make it a process of enabling change. Since personal change is an interior process, the role of the supervisor is to help someone see the need to change. In other words, supervisors no longer climb up on platforms to see more. Rather, supervisors help employees look inside themselves to see more.

When supervision is defined as enabling professional growth, then portfolios take on great usefulness as a tool for supervision. However, not all supervision is directed toward professional growth. Sometimes supervisors in schools must come to the gritty conclusion that a teacher must be fired. The euphemisms abound, of course, but the result is the same: someone's employment at the school ends. When supervision is the process of ending someone's employment, portfolios can be of limited help. A different, tedious process of attention to detail will apply.

Phase I: Project Planning, Recruitment, and Training

Fall   The principal acquires the knowledge of
                                     teaching portfolios necessary to lead
                                     the implementation process.

Spring   The principal recruits a group of likely
                                     prospects to participate in the pilot
                                     project.

                                     The principal identifies and retains
                                     a consulting teacher who will serve as the
                                     project leader.

                                     The project leader confers with pilot
                                     teachers while planning the training
                                     program.

                                     The principal identifies and retains a
                                     program evaluator who is external to
                                     the school.

                                     The program evaluator designs a model
                                     for evaluating the program.

Summer   The project leader conducts the initial
                                     training.

                                     The project leader facilitates the
                                     formulation of rubrics for evaluating
                                     teaching with portfolios in the specific
                                     school community.

                                     Portfolio mentors are identified.

Phase II: The Pilot Year

September   The pilot teachers initiate their
                                     individual teaching portfolios.
                                     Teachers each determine how they will
                                     organize their own portfolios,
                                     conferring with their mentors every
                                     couple of weeks.

October   The pilot teachers identify and begin
                                     collecting possible exhibits they will
                                     include in their respective portfolios,
                                     conferring with their mentors every
                                     couple of weeks.

                                     The project leader meets with the pilot
                                     teachers and facilitates the group's
                                     review of progress, as well as clarifies
                                     concepts and lends advice.

Figure 9.1 *Time line for the implementation of teaching portfolios.*

November	The pilot teachers begin first drafts of reflective statements, sharing the drafts with their mentors.
December	Pilot teachers continue the collection and organization of their exhibits.
February	The project leader meets with the pilot teachers and facilitates the group's review of progress, as well as clarifies concepts and lends advice. Reflective statements are completed, and portfolios begin to take shape.
	The program evaluator reports to principal, project leader, and pilot teachers with formative evaluation data.
March	Pilot teachers complete their portfolios.
April	The project leader meets with the pilot teachers and facilitates the group's presentation of their portfolios to one another.
	Pilot teachers make adaptations to their portfolios, incorporating ideas they may have gained in the presentations to the group.
May	Individual teachers have conferences with the principal, during which they discuss their portfolios and the plans they have made for their professional development.
	Pilot teachers assist the principal in drafting policy that will allow teaching portfolios as an alternative in professional development or teacher assessment programs.
	The principal and the pilot teachers recruit a new group of teachers to participate in the program for the next year.
	Pilot teachers become the mentors for the new teachers.
Summer	New teachers receive training in portfolio assessment of teaching.

Figure 9.1 (continued) *Time line for the implementation of teaching portfolios.*

Phase III: The Expansion Year

Pilot teachers mentor the new teachers, expanding the number of teachers who participate. Teachers developing their portfolios use the same approximate time line as followed in the pilot year.

Phase IV: The Evaluation Year

More teachers are encouraged to participate, and teachers experienced with their own portfolios serve as mentors.

The program evaluator collects data and completes the summative evaluation.

The evaluation helps inform the school community in deciding how teaching portfolios will be used in the future as a tool for professional development.

Figure 9.1 (continued) *Time line for the implementation of teaching portfolios.*

On the other hand, when the purpose of supervision is to enable someone to grow professionally, portfolios are an effective tool. The key for the supervisor is to know the goal of supervision.

Teaching Portfolios as a Tool in Supervision

Once teaching portfolios are instituted as a regular feature of a school's professional development program, they can become a regular feature of the evaluation process. In fact, the portfolio becomes the primary vehicle for communication between the principal and the teacher.

In a typical supervision cycle, the principal meets with a teacher near the beginning of the year to discuss goals and perhaps to plan one or two classroom observations. A final conference usually occurs toward the end of the year. Oftentimes, this cycle is short-circuited and includes only an observation and a final conference.

When teaching portfolios are used in the supervision cycle, the principal meets with the teacher and discusses the teacher's goals, just as before. In addition, the principal discusses how the teacher can show, through the portfolio, progress toward those goals. In brief, the principal becomes another party to the portfolio-planning process. During the course of the year, the principal will still observe instruction and give feedback to the teacher through normal procedures. However, the observations are merely data for inclusion in the portfolio; they are not the evaluation itself. At the end of the year the principal and the teacher confer, using the portfolio as the structure for their conference. They look at the teacher's professional goals and at the evidence of progress toward meeting those goals. Finally, they modify the goals for the next year. The process assumes a spiraling characteristic, and the discussion regarding teaching and learning is set in that teacher's particular context.

SUMMARY

Implementing teaching portfolios as a tool for professional development is a process that cannot be hurried. Mandates from state agencies or district offices with immediate deadlines will impair successful implementation. Instead of bureaucratic proclamation, the best way to implement teaching portfolios is to adopt strategies that emphasize teacher empowerment and program evaluation.

Teaching portfolios are more likely to be accepted by teachers if they are introduced as alternatives to required procedures for teacher evaluation or standard professional development programs. A small group of teachers who begin using teaching portfolios enthusiastically will be the best persuasion for expanded use.

The first group of teachers needs hands-on training to get started. Teachers should develop their portfolios with the guidance of a project leader over an extended period of time. Then, these first few teachers should serve as portfolio mentors to others in the school who want to begin their portfolios.

When teaching portfolios are to be used for the evaluation of teaching, rubrics need to be developed. However, the rubrics should be written at the level closest to the teachers who will be evaluated. Indeed, the implementation process needs to include the collaborative development of rubrics.

Finally, teaching portfolios as a tool for professional development need to be evaluated. Whether the process of teachers engaging in self-evaluation and reflection actually causes professional growth is the central question to be asked in the program evaluation.

The entire process of implementing teaching portfolios in a school community should begin with planning, advance with training, continue with utilization and expansion, and end with evaluation. At least three years should be allowed for implementation to occur.

REFERENCE

Tierney, D. S. (1992). *Teaching portfolios: 1992 update on research and practice.* Berkeley, CA: Far West Laboratory for Educational Research and Development.

Carmen Garcia's Portfolio Items

I. Introduction
   A. Resumé
   B. Autobiography
   C. Samples of own school work
   D. School description
   E. Description of class make-up
   F. *All about Me* page
   G. Class photograph
   H. Reflective statement

II. Influences
   A. Photographs of bulletin boards
   B. Floor plan of classroom
   C. Daily schedule
   D. Photograph of cooperative group
   E. Yearly planning document
   F. Reflective statement

III. Instruction
   A. Brainstorming worksheet
   B. Thematic unit plan
   C. Lesson plan
   D. Student work sample
   E. Videotape
   F. Learning center schedule
   G. Photographs of centers in use
   H. Reflective statement

IV. Individualization
   A. Yearly learning center plans
   B. Learning center
   C. Student card sample
   D. Informal reading inventory sample page
   E. Students' work samples
   F. Reflective statement

V. Integration
   A. Philosophy of education
   B. Evaluations of teaching
   C. Student note
   D. List of goals for improvement
   E. Reflective statement

Gary Donovan's Portfolio Items

I. Introduction
   A. Description of professional assignment
   B. Resumé
   C. Autobiography
   D. Philosophy of education
   E. Teaching certificate
   F. Reflective statement

II. Influences
   A. Photographs of bulletin boards and displays
   B. Content area bibliography
   C. Software bibliography
   D. Overview of computer use in classroom
   E. Reflective statement

III. Instruction
   A. Satire planning document
   B. Satire lesson plan
   C. Student journal entry
   D. Student work samples
   E. Tech prep business community feedback
   F. Yearly computer objectives
   G. Videotape
   H. Reflective statement

IV. Individualization
   A. American literature bibliographies
   B. Student journal pages
   C. Student work sample
   D. Computerized grade-reporting explanation
   E. Reflective statement

V. Integration
   A. Philosophy of education reference
   B. Evaluations of teaching
   C. Student note
   D. Chamber of Commerce award
   E. Letters from business community
   F. List of goals for improvement
   G. Reflective statement

Marianne Miller's Portfolio Items

I. Introduction
   A. School mission statement
   B. Teaching certificate
   C. Resume
   D. Reflective statement

II. Influences
   A. Photographs of bulletin
      boards
   B. Discipline plan
   C. Textbook bibliographies
   D. Reflective statement

III. Instruction
   A. Planbook page
   B. Worksheets
   C. Test scores
   D. Reflective statement

IV. Individualization
   A. Reading group lists with test
      scores
   B. Future teacher list
   C. Test scores
   D. Graded workbook pages

E. Planbook page
F. Reflective statement

V. Integration
   A. Philosophy of education
   B. Evaluations of teaching
   C. Letter of commendation
   D. List of goals
   E. Reflective statement

Sample Rubrics for Portfolio Evaluation of Teaching Using the Five I's Method of Organization

EACH community of teachers should develop its own set of rubrics for evaluating teaching. Only when teachers discuss with one another the meaning of good teaching and they consider the ways that good teaching can be seen through portfolios will they profit fully from developing their own self-portrait as a teacher. With this caveat in mind, a sample set of rubrics for evaluating teaching through portfolios is offered. The hope is that a concrete example will serve as a reference point for groups of teachers to create their own rubrics.

Rubrics should include three elements: the attributes of good teaching, the characteristics of the evidence used to reveal good teaching, and the performance criteria used when the evidence is considered. Variations on these elements are not only possible, they are encouraged. Moreover, the actual descriptors of the professional skills and personal attributes are assumed to be mere departure points for further discussion.

This sample set of rubrics is organized in three sections: Professional Skills and Qualities, Characteristics of Evidence, and Performance Criteria. The section on Professional Skills and Qualities is organized according to the Five I's in order to parallel the exposition in this book on how to develop a teaching portfolio.

PROFESSIONAL SKILLS AND QUALITIES

Introduction

- The teacher understands the characteristics of the school and community.
- The teacher has a contagious enthusiasm for teaching.

- The teacher reveals a pattern of continuous professional growth.
- The teacher is actively involved in community service.
- The teacher has proper professional credentials for the teaching assignment.
- The teacher engages in reflective thinking on personal qualities and experiences relating to effective teaching.

Influences

- The teacher creates an enriched learning environment—one that invites students to actively engage in learning.
- The teacher creates a learning environment that is physically and psychologically safe for students.
- The teacher creates a learning environment that nurtures self-esteem, self-confidence, and self-discipline.
- The teacher creates classroom dynamics that foster a spirit of trust and cooperation.
- The teacher is aware of community resources and makes effective use of them.
- The teacher actively involves the families of students.
- The teacher makes use of a classroom management plan that fosters learning.
- The teacher engages in reflective thinking on the various classroom aspects that could influence teaching.

Instruction

- Classroom practices show a mastery of content and skills relevant to the teacher's professional responsibilities.
- Classroom practices show mastery of a variety of teaching strategies.
- Classroom practices actively engage students in developmentally appropriate and meaningful learning.
- Instructional plans emphasize the acquisition of academic skills essential to future success.
- Classroom practices emphasize critical thinking and problem solving.
- Instructional plans include learning activities that excite students' imaginations.
- Goals set for students are relevant for students and responsible to the future needs of the community and the students.
- Instructional plans integrate multiple disciplines and a variety of learning activities.
- Classroom practices build a community of learners.

- Reflective statement emphasizes thinking about the necessary components of the planning and implementation of high-quality instruction.

Individualization

- Classroom practices reveal a knowledge of human growth and development.
- Classroom practices accommodate individual differences in the talents, interests, learning styles, and abilities of students.
- Instructional plans include learning activities that are relevant to the cultural backgrounds of individual students.
- Assessment techniques reflect a knowledge of current, authoritative educational research.
- Assessment techniques guide instruction of individual students.
- Reflective thinking emphasizes reason for and practices that accommodate the individual needs of students.

Integration

- The teacher has developed a philosophy of education that informs the teacher's educational practice.
- The teacher has a fluent knowledge of current educational theory as evidenced by classroom practices.
- The teacher shows a pattern of interpreting and acting upon previous evaluations of teaching by supervisors, peers, and students.
- The teacher has a professional development plan that guides the teacher's professional growth by means of explicit goals and strategies for reaching those goals.
- The teacher shows the habit of reflective thinking, leading to self-evaluation of what is working and what is not working.
- The teacher collaborates with peers for the advancement of teaching and learning.
- The teacher engages in reflective thinking, which displays analysis and synthesis of the many aspects of good teaching.

CHARACTERISTICS OF EVIDENCE

- The evidence included in the portfolio is the original work of the teacher.
- The evidence included in the portfolio shows the teacher engaged in all the aspects of teaching.

- The evidence included in the portfolio reveals the teacher's ability to organize and interpret the artifacts of teaching.
- The evidence included in the portfolio reveals the quality of the interactions between the teacher and students.
- The evidence included in the portfolio shows the results of teaching, that is, student growth and accomplished goals through authentic assessment.

PERFORMANCE CRITERIA

Substandard Teaching Performance

- There is insufficient evidence in the portfolio to judge the teacher's performance.
- The evidence provided by the teacher reveals classroom practices or instructional techniques that contradict principles on which there is professional agreement.
- Instructional plans, videos of lessons, or assessment instruments reveal inadequate knowledge of the content being taught.
- Either the content or the methods of teaching are inappropriate for the developmental level or abilities of the students.
- Evidence reveals insensitivity to cultural differences, ranges of ability, or social conditions.
- Evidence reveals insensitivity to physical barriers to learning.
- Evidence reveals classroom dynamics that are oppressive or otherwise detrimental to fostering a classroom environment conducive to learning.
- Reflective statements reveal a lack of understanding of the attributes of good teaching.
- Goals for professional growth are missing, or they are superficial.

Adequate Teaching Performance

- Evidence reveals competence in the professional skills; however, artifacts denote teaching that lacks inspiring qualities or superior resourcefulness.
- The pattern of professional growth or indication of a plan for professional growth is adequate but does not reveal a strong commitment to improvement.
- Personal reflection and self-evaluation are evident.
- Qualities of originality and creativity in the design of learning activities are not persistently evident.

Distinguishing Teaching Performance

* Evidence reveals a contagious enthusiasm for teaching and learning.
* Evidence reveals a unique talent and mastery of skill for teaching as seen in student learning.
* Evidence reveals a capacity to nurture, inspire, and challenge students.
* Evidence reveals a professional vitality that synergizes other teachers.
* Evidence reveals originality, creativity, and resourcefulness in the design and implementation of learning activities.
* Evidence reveals exemplary breadth and depth of knowledge permitting interdisciplinary connections in the design of curriculum.
* Evidence reveals expertise in educational theory and current educational practices.
* Personal and professional growth is habitual, self-directed, intentional, and reflective.

THE goal of the supervisory process is to improve the instruction of children. Clinical supervision places the responsibility for improvement on the teacher. Self-correction and self-improvement are central to the process, and professional collaboration with colleagues is essential. The teaching portfolio provides a very natural vehicle for the self-examination so necessary in clinical supervision. The administrator can use evidence presented in the portfolio, in conjunction with regular observations, to assist a teacher in professional growth. This same evidence can be used in the evaluation process to justify personnel decisions.

Each of our three teachers used the portfolio during the supervisory conference at the end of the year with the principal. The administrator also used the items in the portfolio to illustrate ideas for improvement. Let's listen in at the supervisory conferences of Carmen, Gary and Marianne to see how the whole thing turned out.

CARMEN GARCIA'S SUPERVISORY CONFERENCE

Carmen had been going in for her supervisory conference with the principal for years now. It was routine, like going to the dentist. She knew that Bill Prince, her principal, would say what a fine job she was doing. She would mumble something about just wanting to help kids, and the whole thing would be over for another year. Little did she know that this year was going to be different. As Carmen walked into Mr. Prince's office, she noticed that her portfolio was open on his desk.

Bill: Come in, Carmen. I've been looking forward to this. Your portfolio is just a masterpiece—full of good teaching.

Carmen: Thanks, Bill. It was a lot of work. More than I expected. But I learned so much. I couldn't have predicted what I have learned about myself.

Bill: Your teaching unit is so rich, and this student writing from one of your bilingual kids is quite impressive. I see how these kids improve so much in their English skills in your classroom. This card system of assessment is wonderful, too. Do you actually keep a card on each student?

Carmen: Yes, but it becomes second nature. It really helps me keep track where everybody is academically. I was a little concerned when I was putting the portfolio together that some of the academic needs of my kids weren't getting met. My efforts seem a little scattered, and a few of my kids slip through the cracks.

Bill: You are an excellent teacher, and I don't want us to lose sight of that. Still, wanting to meet the needs of all of your students more closely seems like a noble endeavor. What did you have in mind?

Carmen: I want to focus, for the next year at least, on learning what I can about individualization and integrate that into my classroom practice. Maybe I could take a class or a workshop on learning styles or multiple intelligences. And I know that next year I want to set up my classroom to reflect the ways my kids learn.

Bill: Sounds good. Find the workshop you want to attend, and I'll try to find funding. Let me know other ways I can help, too. There are a couple of things I would like to suggest that you do, also. I know you are shy about sharing your expertise, but I need for you to move beyond that a little. New, young teachers need your wisdom, and every teacher in this building could benefit from your expertise in bilingual education. I would like to assign you as a mentor to a rookie teacher next year, and I would like to support your goal of providing a bilingual workshop for teachers during our fall in-service days.

Carmen: Well, OK. I'll do both of those things. But I'll tell you, it's a lot scarier to teach adults than it is to teach children.

Bill: Granted. But you've never struck me as the type to hide from a challenge, Carmen.

In going into this supervisory conference, Bill Prince had three goals. He wanted to affirm Carmen as a strong teacher; he wanted to help Carmen achieve the goals she had set for herself; and he wanted Carmen to assume more leadership roles within the school. Since his goals and Carmen's were similar, the supervisory conference was an easy success.

MARIANNE MILLER'S SUPERVISORY CONFERENCE

Marianne was not looking forward to her end of the year conference with Mr. Prince. The observations he had done in her classroom had not taken place during particularly successful lessons, and Marianne felt he had been overly critical ever since she had arrived at this school. Still, she had been through these evaluations many times, and nothing ever came of them. Sometimes they were a little unpleasant, but when they were over, they were over. Marianne walked into Bill Prince's office expecting more of the same.

Bill: Come in, Marianne, and let's take some time thinking about the past year by looking through your portfolio.

Marianne: Oh, the portfolio! That's one of the reasons I've been so harried this year. It took so much time that I think I sometimes slighted my teaching just to get it done.

Bill: What made it so difficult?

Marianne: I had nothing much to put in it, and it seemed like a waste of time to put in workbook pages and seating charts. Every time I turned around, John was asking me to *reflect* on something. I'm not interested in thinking so much about my teaching. I just want to go in day by day and teach my lessons.

Bill: Marianne, you know I've been concerned for two years now about your teaching. I think your portfolio may be valuable to you yet, if you use it to look clearly at the teacher you've become. Very little of what you do in your class is your own work. It is all borrowed from somewhere else and taught without imagination. That is reflected in your portfolio when you say you have nothing to put into it. And your remarks about not wanting to think about teaching go right back to my concerns that you are not willing to learn and improve as a teacher. These two areas have been my top concerns with you, and your portfolio validates them.

Marianne: Look, I'm in there every day keeping order. I do what is required of me, and I turn in my paperwork on time. What else do you want?

Bill: It isn't enough, Marianne. It isn't enough here. I expect every teacher here to be striving toward excellence. Mediocrity anywhere weakens the whole school. I cannot justify tenure for you at this point. Here is what I can offer you. I'll give you a one-year extension before deciding on tenure. During this coming year, I will expect you to do three things.

(1) Increase your teaching skills overall by visiting other classrooms, taking courses, etc.

(2) Demonstrate your new skills in the classroom in ways that might include designing units, integrating curriculum, developing creative lessons, etc.

(3) Take responsibility for your own improvement by reflecting on what you most want to improve, and set your own goals.

Marianne: I don't think I deserve this. This is a lot of extra work.

Bill: Yes, it is going to take some effort, but it is the only way I can recommend keeping you for another year. After you've done all of these improvements next year, we'll consider the tenure issue again. Give it all some thought. If you decide you want to try it, give me a written plan of action that addresses my major concerns, and we'll talk the whole thing over again. My date to notify the board is April 15, so I'll need your decision before then.

Bill Prince went into his supervisory conference with Marianne with much less eagerness than his conference with Carmen. He knew he had serious reservations about Marianne's teaching and that not gaining tenure was going to be a shock for her. His overall goal for Marianne was to improve her or remove her. He decided, beforehand, to focus on the areas of learning new methods, increasing specific classroom delivery, and taking more responsibility for self-improvement as the three areas that would have the most immediate impact in Marianne's classroom. He hoped she would come back with increased vigor to improve and a strong action plan to support this. However, he also thought there was a chance Marianne would decide to leave rather than do the extra work. Either way, his goal of improving instruction would be met.

GARY DONOVAN'S SUPERVISORY CONFERENCE

Gary's last conference with Dr. McIntyre was last December. Even though he was at his wit's end back then, she had seemed pleased with his progress. Now that the school year was drawing to its close, Gary was proud of what he had accomplished. This conference should bring no surprises, Gary thought, but he still was nervous. He knew where he had to improve, and he was anxious to know how Dr. McIntyre would handle what were certain to be the same concerns.

Dr. McIntyre: Gary! Your portfolio was packed with some great information about your teaching. Let's talk about it. First of all, I need to say that you've done a great job this year. I've seen a lot of beginning teachers, and some have floundered. But you're in the top flight.

Gary: Thanks, Dr. McIntyre. The two different kinds of classes, not to mention the coaching, sort of pulled me in separate directions. At times, I didn't know whether I was coming or going.

Dr. McIntyre: Well, anyone who works in a high school can relate to that, myself especially.

When I looked through your tech prep section in your portfolio, I was most impressed with the originality of your ideas. And by the way, the personnel director of S-O-S Systems mentioned at the Rotary Club luncheon last week that he was very impressed with the employee's manual your class did.

Gary: That was one of those projects that I wanted to stop once I got started. It turned out OK, but the kids found researching all the regulations to be a bit tedious. But when they finished, they seemed pleased.

Dr. McIntyre: Why do you say that you wanted to stop it midstream?

Gary: Oh, I guess I'm exaggerating. But I started that project with one group, about half the class, while I had two other complicated projects going. I unintentionally gave it the short end of my attention until I saw that it was going to flop if I didn't redirect it. Then, when I turned my attention to those kids, I started to lose the others.

Dr. McIntyre: Sure, that's the challenge when you have several cooperative learning projects going at once. But you need to know that, from where I sit, you pulled off a success. It's not often that business execs downtown compliment what we do here. I am accustomed to other kinds of input from them. Even so, what do you plan to do differently?

Gary: Allison and I talked about this very project when we were talking about which tech prep activities to highlight in my portfolio, and we ended up talking about the problems inherent in cooperative learning. You know, I have decided that I want to make this work—cooperative learning, that is. She suggested I spend some time with a science teacher over at Oakley Middle School. It's not my subject, and it's not my grade level, but Allison said this teacher really knows how to organize a classroom so that all the groups are clicking. I said in my portfolio that will be a goal for next year.

Dr. McIntyre: I saw that. I'll be glad to check with the folks over at Oakley to clear the way for you, if you'd like.

Gary, you already noticed for yourself what I intended to suggest to you. You have an abundance of ideas, and I appreciate your willingness to try them. Keeping enough organization so that your group projects accomplish what you intend will improve, now that you know where to go for some ideas.

By the way, I heard also that the tech prep consortium wants you to be a facilitator in the staff development institutes for next year. That's quite a feather in the hat of a new teacher. Are you going to do it?

Gary: Sure! Why not?

Dr. McIntyre: Well, I also happen to know that you're going to be asked to serve as a teaching portfolio mentor next year. Can you handle both? And coaching, too?

Gary: I am willing to try.

Dr. McIntyre: Gary, you have done a great job for us this year. I told you a month ago that you'd be recommended for reappointment. Your students are benefiting, and our school community is benefiting. I just don't want to see you spread yourself too thin. You mentioned in the last section of your portfolio that you have that tendency. All I'd like to ask you to do is be faithful to your statements in that last reflection you wrote.

Gary: Thanks, Dr. McIntyre. I will think about it. Right now, I'm leaning more toward the mentoring.

Dr. McIntyre planned her conference with Gary with two goals in mind. First, she wanted to convey that he did a bang-up job in comparison to other beginning teachers she had known over the years, and she intended to encourage him. But, also, she knew that she had to help him focus his efforts. Gary's strengths were his energy and his creativity, but he would need some help getting his classroom organized. All the time Gary had spent with his portfolio mentor seemed to have been beneficial because he already knew what he had to do.